J.J. Thomas

The Theory and Practice of Creole Grammar

Salzwasser

J.J. Thomas

The Theory and Practice of Creole Grammar

1. Auflage | ISBN: 978-3-84605-606-6

Erscheinungsort: Frankfurt, Deutschland

Erscheinungsjahr: 2020

Salzwasser Verlag GmbH

THE

THEORY AND PRACTICE

OF

CREOLE GRAMMAR.

BY

J. J. THOMAS.

TO BE HAD AT
T. W. CARR, 13, FREDERICK-STREET; AND AT THE BOROUGH COUNCIL SCHOOL, SAN FERNANDO.
PORT-OF-SPAIN:
THE CHRONICLE PUBLISHING OFFICE.

1869.

PREFACE.

As it was at first my intention to dispense with a preface, I inserted here and there, in the body of this Work, such brief expositions of its plan as I thought desirable. Having so done, I cherished the expectation of avoiding the ordeal of self-obtrusion, which an author must pass through in a formal prologue to the public. But my hope of escape was delusive; for the diversity and extravagance of purpose which rumour imputed to me, in connexion with this undertaking, soon made it obvious that I must, in fairness to myself, explain the *motives* which induced me to attempt a work of the kind.

In the course of the linguistic studies with which I occupied my leisure hours, when a Ward-school teacher, at a distant out-station, I turned my attention to our popular *patois*, for the purpose of ascertaining its exact relation to real French; and of tracing what analogies of modification, literal or otherwise, existed between it and other derived ddialects. These investigations, though prosecuted under the disadvantage of a want of suitable books (which as regards Creole was absolute, and as regards French nearly so), were not altogether fruitless. For I managed to discover, at least in part, the true nature and status of the Creole, in its quality of a spoken idiom. Moreover, finding that the Creole, considered in its relation to correct French, exhibits the whole derivative process in actual operation, (and not in fixed

results, as is the case in older and more settled dialects,) I though
that a grammar embodying these facts would be useful, as a basis o
induction and comparison, to Creole-speaking natives who may
desire to study other languages etymologically. Still, it must be
confessed that these opinions would not, of themselves alone,
have induced me to publish this book — a result brought abou
by considerations having a wider and more urgent importance
and bearing upon two cardinal agencies in our social system
namely, Law and Religion. I might have added Education ; bu
as I mean to treat separately of the nullifying effects of the *pato?*
on English instruction among us, I shall say no more on th
matter here.

In the administration of Justice in this Colony, the interpretin
of Creole occurs as a daily necessity. Yet it is notorious that, i
spite of constant practice, our best interpreters, though generally pe?
sons of good education, commonly fail in their renderings, especiall
from Creole into English. No doubt this is owing in some measu?
to the inherent difficulty of translating off-hand, and at the sam
time *exactly*, from one language into another. But in the prese?
case this difficulty has remained wholly undiminished, because o?
interpreters, like everybody else, neglect to study the idiotis?
of the dialect in combination with their English equivalen?
As this omission has been caused partly by the prevalence of
opinion that Creole is *only* mispronounced French, and pa
by the want of some such manual as the present, I m?
bold to submit the illustrations in this treatise, as calculat?
dispel an error which has often been fatal to the interests of the
and to supply a want to whose existence the continuance of
an error is mainly attributable. But if a practical, and a
same time saddening, refutation of the error above described
wanted, it is afforded by the experience of the Catholic
who may be called the natural pastors of the Creole-speaking
That sermons in pure French must convey very vague

to the minds of hearers who know only *patois*, is obvious
from the wide divergences of construction existing between the two
modes of speech, not to mention the richer vocabulary, the synthetic structure, and other matters in which the French asserts its
superiority over the Creole. The inefficiency of communicating instruction in a language only half understood, has long been perceiv-
ed by the priests; and one of them, the Revd. Père Goux, has publish-
ed a Creole Cathechism, to which are prefixed a few grammatical remarks. As the Abbé does not profess to discuss systematically the pe-
culiarities of the dialect, his observations on that point are, of
course, exempt from technical criticism; but I am free to state
that the *patois* of the catechism, being that of Martinique or Guadaloupe, and withal *very* strange, it would scarcely be more intelligible to a Trinidadian than real French. In the present book are
submitted for consideration renderings from the Gospel of St. John,
etc., which I venture to think even the most ignorant among us
would understand.

The above are the considerations which induced my undertaking
this work. I composed it under circumstances the most disadvan-
tageous, having no other materials than a collection which I had
made of *bellairs*, *calendas*, *joubas*, idioms, odd sayings, in fact, everything that I could get in Creole. As regards French, I had but a
few school-grammars and two third-rate dictionaries, at whose
mercy I stood for everything not within my previous knowledge.
Such were my instruments for achieving a confessedly difficult
undertaking, which, moreover, I could prosecute only at nights,
since my days are taken up by far different occupations. From
night to night, during nearly three years, I laboured almost unceas-
ingly at my task; sometimes threading my way with confidence, frequently having to condemn or re-write whole pages, which a chance
remark of a passer-by or closer inquiry had proved erroneous: yet,
though often baffled, I was never discouraged; for I looked forward
to the day when, respectfully submitting to the public this imperfect

Work and its object, I could claim, if not the praise of
cessful authorship, at least the credit of having endeavo
under great disadvantages, to supply a public want.

It remains now for me to record my obligations to Mr. I
Tronchin, Superintendent of the Woodbrook Normal and N
Schools, for the courteous patience with which he revised su
my proof-sheets as I had an opportunity of submitting to him.
Mr. T. W. Carr, my acknowledgements are due for many Dor
can proverbs (some of which, together with other curious me
I could not insert), and the loan of a *Dictionnaire de l'Acad*
without which I should have remained, to the last, at the n
of inferior compilations. Lastly, my gratitude for many valu
suggestions is hereby expressed to my esteemed friend, Mr. I
Alexis, (now of the Tacarigua School,) to whose well-t
intelligence and exemplary disposition, I rejoice to bear this
testimony.

TRINIDAD, APRIL, 1869.

TABLE OF CONTENTS.

PA

PART III.—SYNTAX.

PART IV.—INTERPRETATION—IDIOMS.

CREOLE GRAMMAR.

PART I.

ORTHOËPY AND ORTHOGRAPHY.

ORTHOËPY signifies the right pronunciation of words.

All the nations of the Earth have certain elementary sounds which are common, and others which are peculiar, to their respective languages. Hence it is that in every language there are words as unpronounceable to foreigners as the *Shibboleth* of the Gileadites was to the children of Ephraim. In attempting to pronounce such words, a foreigner will make as near approximations as his vocal habitudes will allow: and when—as in the case of Africans in the West Indies and America—a barbarous nation adopts a foreign speech, these approximations will be a prominent feature in the dialect thus formed. In dealing, therefore, with the Orthoëpy of the Creole, a dialect framed by Africans from a European tongue, our first duty is to notice the operation of the principle above stated.

Under the general term, *mispronunciation,* are included two distinct processes of verbal alteration. In other words, mispronunciation may affect the *quality*, or it may affect the *number* or *order* of the elementary sounds composing a word. In the former case, the result is PERMUTATION or interchange of letters; and in the latter, those various modes of verbal alteration, which, when reduced to writing, are called FIGURES OF ORTHOGRAPHY.

PERMUTATION.

PERMUTATION or interchange of letters may be illustrated by the following familiar instances:—*p*owl, *p*ish, are the words which a Coolie generally utters for *f*owl and *f*ish. This is Permutation, which properly consists in the substitution of one consonantal sound for another that is pronounced by the same organs. In *p*owl, *p*ish, and *f*owl, *f*ish, the interchange is between *f* and *p*, which are labials or *lip*-letters. We see the operation of the same principle in the French *p*oule and its English equivalent, *f*owl. As another instance of Permutation, we may cite the practice common to people of the Leeward Islands to say " mo*d*er," "bro*d*er," "ano*d*er," etc., for mo*th*er, bro*th*er, ano*th*er, etc. Here the interchange is between *d* and *th*, both dentals or *teeth*-letters. Let us now see how this principle prevails in Creole with respect to words from the parent tongue.

The French Alphabet consists of twenty-five* letters, whereof six, namely, *a*, *e*, *i*, *o*, *u*, and *y*, are vowels, and the remaining nineteen are consonants.

VOWEL CHANGES.

The changes of the French vowel sounds observable in Creole, are as follows:

SINGLE VOWELS.

	Creole.	French.	English.
e *(mute)* is changed into é as in	léver	*lever*	to rise
„ „ „ „ „ i „	ritoù	*retour*	return
„ „ „ „ „ „ „	dimâne	*demande*	request
„ „ „ „ „ „ „	rifair	*refaire*	to make anew
„ „ „ „ „ ou „	chouval	*cheval*	horse
„ „ „ „ „ „ „	douvant	*devant*	before
„ „ „ „ „ „ „	seucoû	*secour*	succour
ê *(circumflexed)* „ é „	crépé	*crêpé*	crisped
„ „ „ „ „ „ „	créver	*crêver*	to burst
„ „ „ „ „ „ „	réver	*rêver*	to dream
u „ „ „ „ i „	bossi	*bossu*	humped
„ „ „ „ „ „ „	cochi	*crochu*	crooked
„ „ „ „ „ „ „	défendi	*défendu*	forbidden

* Twenty-six, if we include *w*.

DOUBLE VOWELS.

	Creole.	French.	English.
ai is changed into *é* as in	anglés	*anglais*	English
	jés	*jais*	jet
au „ „ „ *ô* „	* dôte	*autre*	other
	* zépôle	*épaule*	shoulder
eu „ „ „ *è* „	chalèr	*chaleur*	heat
	flèr	*fleur*	flower
	pèr	*peur*	fear
io (in one instance) „ *ié* „ „	viélon	*violon*	violin
oi is changed (a) into oè as in	boète	*boite*	box
	doègt	*doigt*	finger
	toèle	*toile*	cloth
(b) „ oé „	cloéson	*cloison*	partition
	poéson	*poison*	poison
	poésson	*poisson*	fish

CONSONANT CHANGES.

The nineteen consonants may be thus arranged :—

MUTES.	LIQUIDS.	ASPIRATE.	SIBILANTS.
Labials, *b, p, f, v.*	*l, m, n, r.*	*h.*	*s, x, z.*
Gutturals, *c, g, j, k, q* (u).			
Dentals, *d, t.*			

The following are the principal Creole changes of the consonants :
c, q (u), ch (as in *cheat*), *g.*

The gutturals (or *throat*-letters) *c (u)* and *q (u)* are often represented in Creole by a sound not heard in French: by the sound, that is, of *ch* in *chest, chin,* or in the Spanish *chico*—e. g :

Creole.	French.	English.
cнuite	cui*te*	cooked
cнilotte	cu*lotte*	trowsers
cнouler ι	(re)-cu*ler*	to recede
cнinze	qui*nze*	fifteen
mâcнer ι	*marquer*	to mark
bâcнer ι	*(em)barquer*	to embark

NOTA.—*c* is in Creole sounded *g* in *ganif*, for *Fr. canif*, penknife; *galeféter* for *calfater*, to caulk ; *gouroupier* for *croupier*, servant, *Cr.* sycophant.

* For an explanation of the prostheses, see page 17.

ɢ (u).

The sound of *g (u)* is in Creole represented by the sound of *g* as heard in *gipsy*, *ginger ;* etc., a sound akin to that of *ch* in chin, and equally alien to the French language. The following are examples of this transformation :

Creole.	French.	English.
ɢiɢie	*fig*ure	figure
ɢêpe	*guè*pe	wasp
ɢôle	*gueule*	mouth (of any beast).

LIQUIDS.

N.

When followed by *e* or *i* in French words, this letter is usually sounded like the Spanish ñ in Creole. For the sake of convenience, we shall use this character in writing words wherein this sound occurs. The French combination *gn* might have done ; but we believe there is some slight difference in the two sounds ; besides, it is far more convenient, when practicable, to represent simple sounds by simple characters. The following are illustrations of the change of *-ne, ni,* into ñ :

Creole.	French.	English.
feñant	*faineant*	*lazy*
mañèu	*manier*	*to handle*
pañèn	*panier*	basket

R.

Of all sounds in the French language, that of *r* is the least tolerated in Creole. This poor letter so woefully distorted by Mr. FURLONG in *Handy Andy*, meets with similar, and, it may be, worse treatment from pure *Patois* speakers. The gentleman above mentioned discusses "Iwish" politics, and exhorts his coachman to "dwive on ;" a Creole informing you, for instance, of a brother being ill with ague, says : "fouèr moèn tni *fouisson*," the first and last words being meant for "*frère*" and "*frisson*" respectively. This replacement of *r* by *ou* (which is equivalent to *w* in the same position) occurs when the *r* in a French word is preceded by the labials *b,* *f, v,* and followed by any vowel except *o ;* e.g :—

Creole.	French.	English.
bouave	*brave*	brave
bouèche	*brèche*	breach
bouide	*bride*	bridle
pouatique	*pratique*	practice, *Cr.* also customer
pouévinant	*prévenant*	provident
pouix	*prix*	price
fouacasser	*fracasser*	to shatter
fouemî	*frémir*	to shudder
fouisson	*frisson*	ague
voué	*vrai*	true
vouément	*vraiement*	truly

R, if followed by *o*, either is changed or suppressed altogether when it has a consonant before it; e.g.:—

Creole.	French.	English.
fouömaie / fomaie	*fromage*	cheese
foter / fouöter	*frotter*	to rub
cochi / couöchi	*crochu*	crooked

Er at the end of words is changed into *en* as heard in *examen*; etc. This happens when the syllable *er* is preceded by a nasal sound, (*m* or *n*); e. g :

goumèn	(se) *gourmer*	to fight
mènen	*mener*	to conduct
paîlèn	*panier*	basket
sonnèn	*sonner*	to sound

R into L.

callefoû	*carrefour*	*Cr.* any obscure den, hut
deguelper	*deguerper*	to abscond
salvacane	*sarbacane*	pea-shooter

SIBILANTS.

Between vowels, *s* is the same as *z*.
The termination *age* is the same as *azh*.

At the ending of words, the two sounds above noticed are in Creole generally softened into a sort of liquid pronunciation; e. g:

Creole.	French.	English.
caïe	case	house
choïe	chose	thing
langaïe	langage	language

Nota.—*Coriace*, tough, is *coriache* in Creole.

FIGURES OF ORTHOGRAPHY.

Besides the Permutation of letters necessitated, in most cases, by the vocal organisation of the speaker, there are other processes by which the sounds of a language are altered. As before stated, these processes affect the *number*, and sometimes the *order*, of verbal elements, and, when exhibited in writing, form what are called figures of Orthography. We may alter a word, *(a)* by dropping a letter or syllable from its beginning; *(b)* by dropping a letter or syllable from its ending; *(c)* by dropping a letter or syllable from its middle; *(d)* by adding a letter or syllable to its beginning; *(e)* by adding a letter or syllable to its ending; *(f)* by transposing the letters; *(g)* by inserting a letter or syllable.

These various processes are known by the technical names of:—

a.	Aphæresis, *abstraction.*	e.	Paragoge, *addition.*
b.	Apocope, *abcission.*	f.	Metathesis, *transposition.*
c.	Syncope, *abbreviation.*	g.	Epenthesis, *insertion.*
d.	Prosthesis, *apposition.*		

ILLUSTRATIONS.

a. Of Aphæresis, (dropping a letter or syllable from the beginning of a word).

Creole.	French.	English.
valer	a*valer*	to swallow
plicher	é*plucher*	to peel
river	ar*river*	to arrive
bâcher	em*barquer*	to embark
cocher	ac*crocher*	to hang up (on a peg)

b. Of Apocope, (dropping a letter or syllable from the end of a word).

Creole.	French.	English.
travaïe	*travailler*	to work
chétí	*chétif*	lean, sorry, diminutive
baïe	*bailler*	to give
sa	*savent*	know, *Cr.* can

All French words ending in *le* and *re*, preceded by a *consonant*, are pronounced in Creole without the *l* and the *r* ; as,

Creole.	*French.*	*English.*
aimabe	*aimable*	amiable
nòbe	*noble*	noble
sabc	*sable*	sand
sensibc	*sensible*	sensible, tender
càde	*cadre*	a frame
mòde	*modre*	to bite
monte	*montre*	a watch

c. Of SYNCOPE, (dropping a letter or syllable from the middle of a word).

bandôle	*banderole*	Spanish guitar
zépon	*épéron*	spur
châme	*chambre*	chamber, room
pône	*pondre*	to lay, (as a hen, &c.)

d. Of PROTHESIS, (adding a letter or syllable to the beginning of a word).

*n*âme	*âme*	soul
*am*bandonen	*abandonner*	to abandon
*la*salle	*salle*	hall, drawing-room
zétoèle	*étoile*	star
*di*vin	*vin*	wine
*an*gacer	*agacer*	to provoke, tease

e. Of PARAGOGE, (adding a letter or syllable to the end of a word).

coutim*ance*	*coutume*	custom
gêne*ment*	*gêne*	embarrassment, obstacle
mendi*aner*	*mendier*	to beg, (frequentative)
toûna*ïer*	*tourner*	to turn, „
embaras*sement*	*embaras*	embarrassment

f. Of METATHESIS, (shifting the position of the letters in a word).

t*ri*bilent	*turbulent*	turbulent
lin*té*celle	*étincelle*	* spark
zora*gne*	*orange*	orange
archa*gne*	*archange*	archangel
app*ir*voiser	*apprivoiser*	to tame, to polish, &c.

* The French is, curiously enough, from *scintilla*, by the same figure.

g. Of EPENTHESIS, (inserting a letter or syllable in a word).

assob*ouer*	(s') *absorber*	*Cr.* to belabour.
fouisé, (as if		
from frusé)	*fusée*	rocket
plé*santer*	*pésanteur*	weight
pañèn-a-*lanse*	*panier à anse*	a handled basket

THE CREOLE ALPHABET.

The elementary sounds of the Creole being in most cases identica
with those of the French, Creole words may, in general, be spel
with the letters,. and according to the principles of the latter.　But
as there are in Creole articulations not heard in French, we ar
under the necessity of employing foreign characters, or character
with foreign sounds, to represent the articulations referred to.　W
have, under the head of Permutation, indicated that these are
CH (as heard in *chin, cheek,* &c.); G (as heard in *ginger, gipsy)*
and ñ (as in *féñant, mañèn,* &c.): The Creole Alphabet may, there
fore, be said to consist of twenty-nine letters, including *w.*　As t
u, the Creoles always sound it *ou* in the few cases wherein it i
not converted into *i.*

Character.			*Name.*	*Character.*			*Name.*
A	a	...	*ah*	N	n	...	*enn*
B	b	...	*bay*	Ñ	ñ		
C	c	...	*say*	O	o	...	*o*
CH		...	*chay*	P	p	...	*pay*
D	d	...	*day*	Q	q	...	(like *k*)
E	e	...	*a* (as in fate)	R	r	...	*èr*
F	f	...	*eff*	S	s	...	*ess*
G	g	...	*zhay*	T	t	..	*tay*
G		...	*jay*	U	u	...	*ou*
H	h	...	*ash*	V	v	...	*vay*
I	i	...	*ee*	W	w	...	*way*
J	j	...	*zhay*	X	x	...	*iks*
K	k	...	*kah*	Y	y	...	*ee*
L	l	...	*ell*	Z	z	...	*zedd.*
M	m	...	*emm*				

ACCENTS.

There are certain Orthographic signs employed in French to denote modifications in the sounds of vowels.　These signs, known
by the name of accents, are as follow :—

a. L'accent aigu (the acute accent), is placed exclusively ove
e ; as, *été,* been.

b. *L'accent circonflex* (the circumflexed accent), is placed over vowels, chiefly to denote abbreviation; as in

gâter for the old form *gaster*, to spoil

prêter   „   „   „   *prester*, to lend

maître   „   „   „   *maistre*, master

côte   „   „   „   *coste*, coast

flûte   „   „   „   *fluste*, flute

Besides its legitimate use in such French words, this accent is, in course of this Work, placed over *o* whenever this letter has the same sound as in the English *hot, pod;* and over any other vowel that may seem to require it, especially in abbreviated syllables.

c. *L'accent grave* (the grave accent), placed over *e*, as in *père*, *mère.* We use this accent also over the *e* of the converted final syllables *en, er*, to denote the peculiarity of the word-formation in which they occur.

d. *Le trema* (the diæresis), placed over a vowel, denotes its separate pronunciation; as, *waïcou*, (wa-i-cou,) cloth wrapped round the waist.

PRONUNCIATION OF LETTERS.

VOWELS.

a is sounded as in *far.* When circumflexed (â), the sound is somewhat lengthened; as in *pâler*, Fr. *parler*, to speak; *châme*, Fr. *chambre*, room or chamber.

e without any accent is mute, and being so, it is scarcely sounded; as in *cela* (slah,) thát; *tabe*, (tab,) table. When final, *e* mute is not at all heard in ordinary discourse.

i is sounded like *e* in *me;* as in *gibier*, (zhe-be-ay,) bird. When circumflexed (î), this letter has a lengthened sound, as in *vite* (veet,) Fr. *vitre*, glass, (rare in Cr.)

o has the sound of the English *o* in *rote, go;* e. g : *aussitot*, (o-see-toe), soon.

ô (circumflexed) is sounded as in *got, not*, but a little longer; e. g : *môder* (modd-ay,) Fr. *modre*, to bite; *zôtes*, (zott,) Fr. *(vous) autres*, you.

y is pronounced like *i.*

CONSONANTS.

With the exception of *c, f,* and *l,* all the consonants when final are mute, as in French; e. g : *pitit*, (pit-tee,) Fr. *petit*, small; *bas*, (bah,) stocking; etc. In order that a final consonant should 'be sounded, an unaccented *e* is placed after it; as, *vite,* (veet,) quick; *salude,* (sah-ladd,) salt d.

c has the same sounds as in English; viz., *(a)* that of *k,* before *a* and *o; (b)* that of *s,* before *e* and *i;* e.g: *cacoyèr,* (kak-o-year,) a brazen girl; *camisole,* (kam-e-zoll,) jacket; *cévelle,* (sev-ell,) Fr. *cervelle,* brain; *ciseaux,* (see-zo,) scissors. It it written with a cedilla (ç), when, before *a* and *o,* it is to sound like *s;* e. g: *façade,* (fass-add,) frontage; *façon,* (fass-onh,) mode, manner. *c* is heard at the end of *almanac; bec,* (bek,) beak ; *couöc,* (kwok,) Fr. *croc,* crook; *crac,* fib; *estomac,* stomach; *grec,* frank, out-spoken; *bouc,* (book,) ram ; *lac,* lake ; *sac,* bag; *sec,* dry ; *tabac,* tobacco ; *jouc,* (zhook,) Fr. *joug,* yoke. As in French, *c* has the sound of *g* in *second,* and its derivatives.

ch is pronounced like *sh* in English; as *facher,* (fash-ay,) to vex; *tache,* (tash,) task.

CH, in course of this work, must be sounded as in the English words *chat, cheat, chin;* e.g : *babou*CH*ette,* (bab-boo-chett,) a rope-halter ; *pi*CH*ette,* (pe-chett,) a stake.

d has the same sound as in English; except that, according to rule, it is not heard at the end of words.

f is sounded as in English; at the end of words it is generally heard. The following are the cases in which *f* final is silent :— *zéfs,* (zay,) eggs; *béfs,* (bay,) oxen, as in " *moulin à béfs.*" These are Creole corruptions of (*des*) *œufs,* (*ües*) *bœufs,* in which words the *f* is not sounded.

g before *a* and *o* is pronounced as in English ; e.g: *gâter,* (gatt-ay,) to spoil; *gogo,* name-sake. When followed by *e* and *i,* it must be sounded like *zh;* e.g : *age,* (azh,) age; *loger,* (lo-zhay,) to lodge; *gibier,* (zhe-be-ay,) bird.

G must in all cases be pronounced like the English letter *j,* or like *g* in *gipsy, ginger;* e.g : ba*G*ette, (bah-jet,) Fr. *baguette,* a ramrod.

h is sometimes silent, as in *habit,* (ab-ee,) coat ; *harassé,* (ar-ass-ay,) bothered out ; and sometimes aspirated, as in *hareng,* (har-anh,) herring ; *haï,* (hah-yee,) to hate ; etc.

j is always sounded like *zh;* e.g : *jène,* (zhenn,) Fr. *jeune,* young; *jimeau,* (zhim-o,) Fr. *jumeau,* twin.

k has the same sound as in English.

l is pronounced as in English, and heard at the end of words, except in the following: *fisil*, (fiz-ee,) Fr. *fusil*, gun ; *baril*, (bar-ee,) barrel; *gentil*, (zhan-tee,) decent; *zoutil*, (zoo-tee,) Fr. *outil*, tool, etc.

m and *n* are pronounced as in English when they begin a word or syllable, or come between two vowels; but at the end of words they have a much duller sound; in fact, they only impart nasality to the vowel preceding; as in *bon*, good; *faim*, hunger; *chien*, dog.

p is silent in *corps*, (cor,) body; *compter*, (con-tay,) to reckon ; *dompter*, (don-tay,) to subdue; *temps*, (tanh,) time; *drap*, (drah,) cloth, sheet, etc.

ph is pronounced *f* as in English.

q (*u*) has the sound of *k*; e.g : *quitter*, (kit-tay,) to quit; *quolibet*, (ko-lib-bet,) tittle-tattle.)

r, when heard at all, has a most peculiar sound, which no English letters can represent. When final, it is never sounded in Patois.

s has two sounds : one as in *salvation*, *soberness ;* and the other like *z*, as in *ease*, *those.* It is sounded as in the latter instance when it is between two vowels; e.g : *savoèr*, Fr. *savoir*, knowledge; *simaine*, Fr. *semaine*, a week; *ouösair*, (wo-zèh) Fr. *rosaire*, rosary; *poser*, (po-zay,) Fr. *reposer*, to rest. When final, *s* is silent, except in *plis* (sometimes pron. *pliss*), Fr. *plus*, more; *vis*, (viss,) a screw, etc.

t has generally the same sound as in English; but when it would in English be sounded *sh*, as in *patient, nation*, etc., it is, according to French orthoëpy, pronounced *se ;* e.g : *patient*, (pah-se-anh); *nation*, (nah-se-onh), etc.

In *th*, only the *t* is sounded ; e.g : *dithé*, (de-tay,) Fr. *(du) thé*, tea; *théate*, (tay-att), Fr. *théatre*, theatre, etc.

t final is heard in *bout*, (boot,) end, cigar; *bouit*, (bwitt,) Fr. *brut*, rough; *dôt*, (dott,) Fr. *dot*, dowry; *doègt*, (dwett,) Fr. *doigt*, finger; *chouvalet*, (shu-val-ett,) Fr. *chevalet*, wooden horse; *chiquet*, (shick-ett,) driblet.

ct is silent in *respect*, (res-pay), respect; but it is sounded *k* in *correct*, (côr-ek,) correct; *direct*, (de-rek,) direct; *exact*, (eg-zak), etc.

v and *w* have the same sound as in English ; e.g : *viêlon*, (ve-aylonh,) Fr. *violon*, violin ; *ridagne*, Fr. *ridange*, <u>lees</u> ; *caïcou*, waist-cloth ; *cangou*, (wanh-goo,) a paste of boiled corn meal.

x has *four* different sounds : *(a)* like *ks*, as in *Alexáne*, (ah-leks-ann,) Fr. *Alexandre*, Alexander ; *(b)* like *gs*, as in *exécice*, (egz-ay-seece,) Fr. *exercice*, exercise ; *(c)* like *s* in *six* (seece,) six ; *dix* (deece,) ten ; *(d)* like *z*, as in *dixième*, (deez-e-emm,) tenth ; etc.

y, at the beginning of words, and *z* are sounded as in English.

ORTHOGRAPHY.

By Orthography is meant the correct representation of articulate sounds by means of written signs. The Orthography of the Creole presents great difficulties, especially with regard to the Verbs. This arises from the fact that it is generally but *one* part of a French verb that has been taken into the dialect, and made, by means of auxilliary words, to express all the modifications of Person, Mood, and Tense. Now, as several parts of a French verb may have the same pronunciation, it is not easy to decide in all cases which of these parts it is that has been adopted. Under the head of Verbs, the reader will see how we have met this difficulty. That our theory is correct seems conclusive from the evidence there brought forward. Should any one object to our spelling all verbs of the first French Conjugation with *er*, as a general rule, he will please to examine such verbs as *coude*, *repóne*, *senti*, etc., which are permanent Creole forms, and at the same time undoubted representations of the original infinitives *coudre*, *repondre*, *sentir*, etc.

With respect to the Orthography of such verbs as the following, however, there may be some difference of opinion :

té which represents the Fr.	*étais*, (*était*,) was
sé ,,	,,	,,	*serais*, (*serait*,) should (be)
vlé ,,	,,	,,	*voulez*, (*voulais*, *voulait ?*) wish
fau' ,,	,,	,,	*faut*, must
pé ,,	,,	,,	*peux*, (*peut*,) can
doé ,,	,,	,,	*dois*, *doit*, (*devez ?*) ought

In spelling most of these, another plan might have been adopted ; viz., to give to each person a specific form representing, at the same time, the correct pronunciation ; e.g :—

1. *moèn péx* in imitation of Fr.	1. *je peux*
2. *ous péz* ,, ,, ,,	2. *vous p(ouv)ez*
3. *li pél*, etc. ,, ,, ,,	3. *il peut*, etc.

But, besides being contrary to the genius of the Creole, which delights in permanent forms, this plan would have reduced us to the shift of employing the same inflections for the plural; besides giving rise to a thousand other difficulties and inconsistencies.

We have, in all cases, endeavoured to follow analogy in writing Patois words. When the French itself failed, the practice of some one or other of the allied languages has been our guide; and when, as it sometimes happened, we could get no assistance from either of these sources, we have carefully analysed the sound and done our best to reproduce it.

ACCENTUATION AND UNION OF WORDS.

Accent is the raising or lowering of the voice in pronouncing certain syllables. In Creole, as in French, the tonic accent is far less marked than in English. But the general rule of French accentuation—namely, that the stress should be laid on the syllable last pronounced—is pretty much the same in the Patois.

It is customary in reading or speaking French to sound final consonants on vowels succeeding them; e.g : *ton ami*, (ton-nam-ee,) thy friend ; *des hommes avares*, (dè-zomm-zavahr,) avaricious men ; " *venez ici*," *dit-il*, (v'nè ze-see, de-teel,) "come here," said he: etc. As Creole is an uncultured speech, whatever of such euphonic refinements it contains is the result of accident and mechanical imitation. For we find that phrases borrowed verbatim from the French, preserve, in general, the modifications of sounds resulting from the concurrence of vowels and consonants; while in constructions that are purely dialectic, hiatusses are by no means unfrequent. The following Patois sentence affords at once illustration and proof of this:—*Fau(t) ous fair yon arangement épis 'i*, pronounced : *Fo ooh fèh yonh ar-anzh-manh ay-pee ee* (you must make an arrangement with him). The reader will remark that of the four hiatusses in the above pronunciation, not one is unavoidable ; but we Creoles pay small attention to the powers of consonants before vowels. It is true that in conversation we mince a few terms ; but, on the whole, our decided preference is for words in their normal condition.

Part II.

—

ETYMOLOGY.

— Etymology treats of individual words, their classifications and accidents. All the words of the Creole dialect may be arranged in nine clasess; viz: 1. Articles; 2. Nouns; 3. Adjectives; 4. Pronouns; 5. Verbs; 6. Adverbs; 7. Prepositions; 8. Conjunctions; 9. Interjections.

ARTICLES.

An Article is a word used with a Noun, to show whether such Noun is to be taken in a general or in a particular sense.

There are two Articles in Creole: *yon*—a, an, Indefinite; and *la* —the, Definite.

THE INDEFINITE ARTICLE.

The Creole Indefinite Article *yon* is invariable; that is to say, it never changes, like the French Indefinite Article (which is sometimes *un* and sometimes *une*), to indicate the gender of the Noun it refers to; e.g.:

Creole.	*English.*	*French.*
yon *çâvolant*	a kite	un *cerf-volant*, masc.
yon *maîte*	a master	un *maître*, ,,
yon *banc*	a bench	un *banc*, ,,
yon *zoragne*	an orange	un *orange*, ,,
yon *macaque*	a monkey	un *singe*, ,,
yon *madame*	a woman, lady	une *dame*, fem.
yon *sésé* / yon *sèr*	a sister	une *sœur*, ,,
yon *matante* / yon *tantante*	an aunt	une *tante*, ,,
yon *plime*	a pen	une *plume*, ,,
yon *zassictte*	a plate	une *assiette*, ,,

THE DEFINITE ARTICLE.

Besides being invariable, *la*, the Creole Definite Article, has the additional peculiarity of coming always *after* its Noun; e.g:

Creole.	*English.*	*French.*
missier la	the man, gentleman	le *monsieur*, masc.
chouval la	the horse	le *cheval* ,,
pouête la	the priest	le *prêtre* ,,
chèpentier la	the carpenter	le *charpentier* ,,
mam'selle la	the young lady	la *demoiselle*, fem.
relizièse la	the nun	la *réligeuse* ,,
lasalle la	the hall	la *salle* ,,
lupoussièr la	the dust	la *poussière* ,,

It must not, however, be supposed that the Creole article, because one in form and sound with the French *la*, is identical with it, and only placed differently with regard to Substantives. On such a supposition, it would be difficult, nay impossible, to account satisfactorily for such combinations as *la-salle la*, *la-glacièr la*, and a host of others, in which the French article, *la*, however otherwise misused, is nevertheless in its usual place *before* the noun. The origin of the Creole *la*, and, incidentally, of its peculiar construction, must therefore be sought elsewhere. In fact, this *la* of ours is simply the French adverb of place, *là*, as found in *ce-banc-là*, *ce-verre-là*, and similar expressions. In uttering the two phrases cited above, a Frenchman makes but *two* sounds for each; viz: *sbanc-là*, and *sverre-là*. The first word, *ce*—a mere sibilation—escaping an untutored ear, *sbanc-là* and *sverre-là* would appear *banc-la* and *verre-la* respectively: hence the Creole usage. But it may be objected that *ce banc-là* oftener means *that* bench, than *the* bench; and the same of *ce verre-la*, *that* glass, &c. To this we reply: first, that, in many cases, it is not easy to discriminate between *that* and *the*, especially in French; and secondly, that the demonstrative sense of such phrases has been subordinated in Creole on the same principle according to which the primary import of *ille*, *illa*, has been modified on passing into the French *le*, *la*.

NOUNS.

Nouns or Substantives are the names by which we designat
Persons, Animals, Places, or Things; as *gouroupier*, sycophant
babiche, alligator; *ville*, town; *wanga*, sorcery.

The majority of Nouns in Creole are French; but there are. som
peculiar to the dialect, and others borrowed from English an
Spanish. We therefore arrange them under four heads, the first
which shall, for the sake of convenience, be divided into two section

FRENCH NOUNS IN CREOLE.

a. Nouns taken and used *individually*, with or without chang
of pronunciation :—

Creole.	English.	French.
balyé	broom	balai
baton*	stick	
bijou	jewel	
boutique	shop	
bouton	button	
carême	dry season	
châme	chamber, room	chambre
côbêïe	basket	corbeille
coton	cotton	
danger	danger	
dési	desire, wish	désir
doulèr	pain	douleur
empèchement	hindrance	
envie	desire	
fontaine	fountain	
foûchette	fork	fourchette
gant	glove	
geounou	knee	genou
grîe	grating, gridiron	grille
hades / rades	clothes	hades
jalousie	jealousy	
jambon	ham	
lagon	lagoon	

* When the word has not been altered at all, we leave the French colum
blank, allowing the reader to see the French in the Creole.

Creole.	English.	French.
liçon	lesson	*leçon*
mâmite	camp-kettle	*marmite*
ménage / *menaïə*	domestic affairs, furniture	
misèr	trials, distress	*misère*
nage	swimming, rower	
nez / *nèn*	nose	*nez*
objection / *ôjection*	objection	*objection*
papier	paper	
pantoûffe	slipper	*pantouffle*
ravaïe	ravage	*ravage*
racine	root	
rideau	curtain	
séson	season	*saison*
simaine	week	*semaine*
temps	time	
vache	cow	

b. Nouns that have been taken *"in construction."*

This section will comprise Nouns taken into Creole in combination with some other word, usually an article or an adjective, which, having lost all meaning of its own, is become a mere initial of the newly-formed substantive. This incorporation of words that are " in construction" is not peculiar to the Creole. If we take, for example, the French *Monsieur*, sir, gentleman, we find that its component parts are *mon*, an adjective — my, and *sieur*, a noun — sir, master, &c. Literally, therefore, *mon-sieur* is *my*-master, *my* sir, or the like. But *mon* having lost all significance here, the combination *mon-sieur* means only what was formerly expressed by *sieur* alone. As with *mon*, in this particular instance, so has it fared with *du, des, la, le, ma, mon, ses, un (une)*, which, generally in an altered shape, form the initial of many Creole substantives beginning with *di, la, l, ma, moun, ses, n* and *z :* the two last letters indicating the initial sounds of French words beginning with a vowel or silent *h*, immediately preceded by *un (une)* and *des,*

les, &c. Subjoined are specimens of these composite **nouns**, wi
such locutions as may have given rise to them :

Creole.	English.			French.		
difé	fire,	originated	from	du *feu*,	lit.	*some* fire
dithé	tea,	„	„	du *thé*,	„	*some* tea
divin	wine,	„	„	du *vin*,	„	*some* wine
dleau	water,	„	„	de l'*eau*,	„	*some* water
labitide	habit,	„	„	l'*habitude*,	„	*the* habit
lâdoèse	slate,	„	„	l'*ardoise*,	„	*the* slate
lintécelle	spark,	„	„	l'*étincelle*,	„	*the* spark
lafiéve	fever,	„	„	la *fievre*,	„	*the* fever
lapôte	door,	„	„	la *porte*,	„	*the* door
lageôle	jail,	„	„	la *géole*,	„	*the* jail
mounonque ⎫ mounonc ⎬ uncle, „ „				*la* gêole, „ *the* jail mon *oncle*, „ *my* uncle		
mononque ⎭						
madame*	lady,	„	„	ma *dame*,	„	*my* lady, *Mrs.* (appellativ
matante	aunt,	„	„	ma *taute*,	„	*my* aunt
sesadiex	farewell, leave-taking ⎫		„	ses *adieux*,	„	*his* leave-taking
nâme	soul,	„	„	une *ame*,	„	*a* soul
nannée	year,	„	„	une *année*,	„	*a* year
ninîme	riddle,	„	„	une *enigme*	„	*a* riddle
nômme	man,	„	„	un *homme*,	„	*a* man
zaffair	business,	„	„	des *affaires*	„	*certain* affairs
zagriñen ⎫ zariñen ⎬	spider,	„	„	des *araigné*,	lit.	*some* spiders
zaile	wing,	„	„	des *ailes*,	„	*some* wings
zallimette	lucifer match,		„	des *allumettes*,	lit.	*some* matches
zamas	Cr. canetops,		„	des *amas*,	„	*some* heaps
zamis	friends,	„	„	des *amis*,	„	*some* friends
zampoule	tumour,	„	„	des *ampontes*,	lit.	*some* tumours
zanɢie	fresh water eel,		„	des *anguilles*,	„	*some* eels
zanana	pine apple,		„	des *ananas*,	„	*some* pine apples
zanneau	ear-ring,	„	„	des *anneaux*,	„	*some* ear-rings
zagne, (rare)	angel,	„	„	des *anges*,	„	*some* angels
zassiette	plate,	„	„	des *assiettes*,	„	*some* plates
zêbe	grass,	„	„	des *herbes*,	„	*some* herbs

✷ The French use the phrase, "*faire* la *madame*," to set up for a lady.

Creole.	English.			French.		
zéboueie	fish-gill, „		„	(les *ouïes,)*	„	*the* gills
zécôce	bark, (of a tree)	„		les *écorces,*	„	*the* barks
zéCHime, (léCHime)	skimmings,		„	des *écumes,*	„	*some* froth
zéffort	effort, „		„	des *éfforts,*	„	*some* efforts
zéGuie	needle, „		„	des *aiguilles,*	„	*some* needles
zentraies	entrails, bowels		„	des *entrailles,*	„	*the* bowels
zépinâd	spinage, „		„	des *épinards,*	„	*some* spinage
zépingue	pin, „		„	des *épingles,*	„	*some* pins
zépôle	shoulder, „		„	les *épaules,*	„	*the* shoulder
zépon	spur, „		„	des *éperons,*	„	*some* spurs
zôdie	sweepings, dirt,		„	des *ordures,*	„	*some* sweepings, &c.
zoragne	orange, „		„	des *oranges,*	„	*some* oranges
zoreie	ear, „		„	les *oreilles,*	„	*the* ears
zos	bone, „		„	des *os,*	„	*some* bones
zôteî	toe, „		„	les *orteils,*	„	*the* toes, &c.

To the same class belong *Bondié*, God, or a deity of any kind; as, *yon* bondié *bois,* a wooden god; *beautemps,* good weather, (which is often preceded by a qualificative; as, belle *beautemps,* joli *beautemps,* fine weather); *bonmatin,* morning; *yon joú bonmatin,* one day (in the) morning; *dóte* for *d'autre; zótes* for *vous autres;* etc. are formed an the same principle.

NOUNS PECULIAR TO THE DIALECT. [*]

Here we include not only those nouns whose origin is local or African, but those also that have been framed by the Creoles from French words. The following specimens are but a few :—

Creole.	English.	French Etymology.
amblouï	evasion	
baboule	a kind of drum dance	
bacou-bacou	perquisites, secret gains	
bamboula	a kind of dance	

---

[*] It is not pretended that some of the words of which the etymology has not been given or suggested, may not be French or Spanish: what we mean is, that none of them ever occurred in the French and Spanish works that we have consulted.

Creole.	English.	French Etymology.
bébelle	a toy, finery	(*belle*)
boubou	a fright, hobgoblin	
boucan	a hurdle for smoking meats, a pile of sticks for burning; a row	
boûgonnemcnt	a grumbling, a murmur	(*bourdon ?*
boulôque	confusion	
bouzin, brouzin	a hastily got up dance	
caïambouque	any secret place, obscurity	
camañoc	sweet cassada	(*manioc*)
chavirade	an upturning	
cиiribibi	a powder of parched maize	
choubichou	talisman, amulet, sorcery	
coscaie	manioc farina mixed with syrup	
eotiche	sandal, mocassin	
coucou	a calabash bored at an end and hollowed out	
couyenade *couyonade*	nonsense, trifling	
déchirade	a tearing	(*déchirage*)
développade	a thrashing	(*développer*)
décirade	a turning back	(*dévier*)
drivaïèr	a rover, vagabond	(*dériver*)
fanfouliche	tinsel ornament	
fiñolemcnt *fiolement*	a refining	(*fignoler*)
gabl	a bundle of thatch leaves	
gaïape	a rude feast given to gratuitous helpers in field work	(*gaillard ?*)
gigodine	furbelows, any dress ornamentation	
Gioli	effects	
graffiñade	a scratching	(*griffade*)
happe-salade	a meddler	(*happer,* etc.)
horrôpe	a scrape, difficulty	
iche	child	
joupa, ajoupa	a garden hut, cabin	

Creole.	English.	French Etymology.
maconage maconaïe	a clumsy sewing or tying	
malongue	a fellow passenger from Africa	
malté	distress, destitution	(mal)
matété	farina boiled into pap	
mingan	anything smashed	
mou-mou moun-moun	a dumb person	
negue-maite	lit. a slave of the same owner; a butting with the head	(nègre maître)
ouäche	display in dress or behaviour	
sainbleau	a heavy shower	
savonade	a soaping	(savon)
soucrade	a shaking	(secouer)
soucouïan	a blood-sucking wizard	
talalà	fuss, to-do	
tambì	a row, rambling talk	
tantamâ	(Sp. tanta mar ?) great fuss	
témécou	anything that embarasses	
touloume touroume	a coarse kind of sugar cake	
toural tourìal	a talismanic leaf	
toûnement	a turning	(tourner)
virement	(with the foregoing), a twisting	(virer)
vonvon	a bee	
vonvonnement	a buzzing	
waïà	a sort of hamper carried on the back	
zandoli	lizard	
zengouinGin	sorcery, jugglery	

ENGLISH NOUNS IN CREOLE.

The English Nouns used in Creole are very numerous. They relate chiefly to matters brought into the Colony, or more directly under Creole cognizance, through English agency. The following will indicate the nature of these terms : *bosine,* (bo-sinn,) boatswain (mill overseer); *stime-ingine,* steam-engine ; *man-a-wâr,* man-of-war ; *mèl-bôte,* mail-boat ; *wâdine,* warden ; *warrant ; tramway ;* &c., &c.

The wayward fancifulness of our people has not suffered' the English portion of their dialect to remain without some perversions of meaning. As examples, we may notice the words "blanket," "blow," and "tune." "*Blankite*" in the mouth of a Creole, does duty similar to that done by "*nigger*" in the lips of a person proud of his exemption from the "curse of Canaan:" that is to say, *blankite* is a term of reproach levelled at *fair* complexions, especially. when *rosiness* forms no part of them.

As to "*blow*," it is an incident or anecdote ; e.g : *yon* blow *sôtî river la-bas là*, an incident has just happened yonder ; *ba nous* blow *missier la, nonc, machèr*,—pray, tell us the story about the gentleman,. my dear.

A "*tune*," under the Creole form CHO*une*, is by no means suggestive of harmony. On the contrary, it denotes every provocation by which one seeks to fasten a quarrel upon another ; as, *Main ça yon* CHO*une !* what a quarrel-picking! Sometimes a quarrel itself is thus described ; as, *cosquel la té tinî yon bellè* CHO*une épîs yeaux*, that ridiculous fellow had a fine row with them, Fr. *Ce ridicule-là avait une dispute sérieuse avec eux.*

NOUNS FROM THE SPANISH*.

From the ancient owners of the Colony, and doubtless from intercourse with the Main, our dialect has derived many Spanish words ; whereof the following Nouns are among the most common :—

Creole.	*English.*	*Spanish Etymology.*
arèpe		
babouchette	a rope muzzle	(*boca ?*)
bôï	indian corn dumpling	(*bollo*)
cabouïà	a noose	(connected with *cabestro*).
cachape	a biscuit made of ground corn	
catà	a sauce or syrup made of manioc juice	(*catar*)
consuèl	consolotion, remedy	(*consuelo*)
cosquèl	a laughing stock	(*cosquillas*)

---

* Many of our words belong to the popular dialect of the Spanish Main, with which our acquaintance is, unfortunately, very limited. The reader will please observe that *ch* in this section is pronounced as in *chin, cheat,* &c.

Creole.	English.	Spanish Etymology.
couyane	the wife or husband of one's countryman or country-woman	(cuñada)
farimañèl	ostentation, braggadocio, finery	(faramallerd)
golète	schooner ; Cr. also a long pole	(goleta)
manià	rope fetters put on horses	(maniatar ?)
matapèl	ant-eater	(matar, perro)
morocôte	a river fish ; a coin, value $20	
morocoï	land turtle	
papèlon	brown sugar (ungraulatend) made in loaves	(pabellon ? from the shape of the article ?)
pélăo	a savoury dish of rice, fowl, &c. boiled together	(paladar ?)
sancoche	a coarse dish of beef and plantains	(sancochear)
sapatèr	a flat fish	(zapatero)
sogue	thongs	(soga)
tassò	dried beef	(tasajo)
tembandol | tembladol ⎰	electric eel	(tembladur)
torète	a bullock	(toreto)

NUMBER.

There are two Numbers : the Singular, denoting one object ; and
the Plural, denoting more than one.

As regards spelling, the plural of Nouns (and Adjectives) may
be formed, as in French, by adding *s ;* except when the Singular ends
in *s, x,* or *z,* in which case there is no addition ; e.g :

	Creole.	English.	French.
Sing.	yon zanana	a pine apple	un anana
Pl.	yon pile zananas	many pine apples	plusieurs ananas
Sing.	yon lapôte	a door	une porte
Pl.	déx, tois lapôtes	two, three doors	deux, trois portes
Sing.	yon gouös caïe	a large house	une grande maison
Pl.	grands caïes	large houses	(de) grandes maisons

Nouns and Adjectives ending in *s, x,* and *z.*

	Creole.	English.	French.
Sing.	yon mauvés zos	a bad bone	un mauvais os
Pl.	mauvés zos	bad bones	(de) mauvais os
Sing.	lavoéx doux la	the sweet voice	la voix douce
Pl.	yon pile nez	many noses	plusieurs nez

Nouns ending in *au, eau* may add an *x* according to French usage; e.g :

	Creole.	English.	French.
Sing.	*yon bateau*	a sloop	*un bateau*
Pl.	*commèn bateaux ?*	how many sloops?	*combien de bateaux ?*

But, as this is a *spoken*, and not a *written* dialect, we must attend more particularly to the *oral* mode of expressing Number.

The Singular is shown, as in English and French, by means of the Article Indefinite : of this there are sufficient examples above.

Moèn voèr zanneaux *et-pîs* bouacelets *nans yon magazin,* I saw *ear-rings* and *bracelets* in a store. In this sentence, no Article is used before *zanneaux* (ear-rings), and *bouacelets* (bracelets); because they are indeterminate, and denote the primary perception. But if we continue the sentence, adding our opinion of what we saw in the store, we must employ the article; as, *ces zanneaux* la *té bien nans goût moèn; main moèn pas té content ces bouacelets* la, *the* ear-ring were much to my taste; but I did not like *the* bracelets. We use the definitives *ces-la, (the)* in these instances, because *zanneaux* and *bouacelets* have, by the second mention of them, become determinate and specific. The rule for the Plural may, therefore, stand thus : — that, in the case of indeterminate objects, it is denoted by employing the Noun without any Article; as, *I tint* mangos *et-pîs* chapoties *nans pañèn la,* there are *mangoes* and *sapodillas* in the basket. But when the object spoken of is determinate, *ces* is put before the Noun, and *la* after it; as, *ous pé pouend* ces *chapoties-la, main léssez* ces *mangos-la là, pâce moèn bisoèn yeaux,* you may take *the* sapodillas, but leave *the* mangoes there, for I want them. All this is in accordance with Creole and English usage; but French usage is difrent. In the case of indeterminate objects, when no words denoting quantity come before the Noun, the partitive article *must* be used; e.g : *J'ai vu dans un magazin* des *anneaux et* des *bracelets ;* les *anneaux étaient bien à mon goût, mais* les *bracelets ne me plaisaient pas.* The Creole plural is simply the French demonstrative construction, which, in familiar style, is frequently used in cases of this kind.

GENDER.

In French Grammar there are only two Genders, which are applied to all Nouns, whether denoting animate or inanimate objects. As regards the latter class of Nouns, the Gender assigned them by custom is indicated by inflecting the Articles, Adjectives, and Pronouns relating to them. But, as in Creole Pronouns do not vary for Gender, and Articles do not vary at all, it is in connexion with the Adjectives, which admit, though sparingly, of such variation, that the Gender of nouns denoting lifeless objects can be best determined. We therefore defer remarking on the subject till we come to treat of Adjectives. Meanwhile, it may be here recorded that Patois-speakers, when imitating the French construction, employ the feminine article, *la*, before the following substantives, although in French they are, in fact or by analogy, of the Masculine Gender :—

Creole.	*English.*	*French.*
la *badinaie*	joking	le *badinage*
la *blâme*	blame	le *blame*
la *bouffaie* *	food	
la *bouigandaie*	*Cr.* romping, &c.	le *brigandage*
la *contentement*	joy, gladness	le *contentement*
la *diraie*	duration	(la *durée)*
la *restant*	remainder	le *restant*

We turn now to the Gender of Nouns denoting *animate* objects. The distinction of sex in Creole is indicated in three ways: *(a)* By different words; *(b)* by composition; *(c)* by derivation. *a* By different words; as,

	Creole.		*English.*		*French.*
Masc.	Fem.	Masc.	Fem.	Masc.	Fem.
compèr	*macoumèr*	godfather	godmother of one's child	*compère*	*commère*
coq	*poule*	cock	hen		
crabier	*gasset*† (Sp).	heron		*crabier*	

* The termination *age* (whence the Creole *aïe)* is usually masculine in French.

† This word is the Spanish *garza*, a heron. In fact we say in Creole, *gasse à morène*, evidently *garza morena*, brown heron. It needs scarcely be added that the Creole form of the expression involves no reference to the colour of the bird.

Creole.		English.		French.	
Masc.	Fem.	Masc.	Fem.	Masc.	Fem.
fouèr	*sêr, sésé*	brother	sister	*frère*	*sœur*
gâçon	*fìz*	boy, son	girl, daughter	*garçon*	*fille*
louoi	*lareine*	king	queen	*roi*	*reine*
mari	*femme, madame* }	husband	wife	*mari*	*épouse*
missier	*madame*	gentleman	lady	*mousieur*	*madame*
mounonque	*matante, tantante* }	uncle	aunt	*oncle*	*tante*
nivé	*nière*	nephew	niece	*neveu*	*nièce*
nomme	*femme*	man	woman	*homme*	*femme*
tauoueau	*vache*	bull	cow	*taureau*	*vache*
torète (Sp.)	*ginisse*	bullock	heifer	*jeune taureau*	*genisse*

b   By composition or the compounding of words ; as,

Masc.	Fem.	Masc.	Fem.	Masc.	Fem.
mâle-codêne	*fimelle-codêne*	turkey-cock	turkey-hen	*dindon*	*dinde*
bouc-cabouite	*fimelle-cabouite*	he-goat	she-goat	*bouc*	*chèvre*
macou-chatte	*fimelle-chatte*	tom-cat	she-cat	*chat*	*chatte*

When it is wished to intimate that the female has had young,
maman is prefixed instead of *fimelle,* especially when the feminine
has not a distinctive form :—

Creole.	English.	French.
yon maman-bououique	a she-donkey	*une anesse*
yon maman-chatte	a she-cat	*une chatte*
yon maman-chein, ,, ,, *chien* }	a bitch	*une chienne*
yon maman-codêne	a turkey-hen	*une poule d'Inde,* &c.,

and so on of animals, with the above restriction.

c   Gender is also shown by derivation ; as,

Creole.		English.		French.	
Masc.	Fem.	Masc.	Fem.	Masc.	Fem.
*câpe**	*cabouesse*	(cob	cobress)	*(capre*	*capresse)*

* The English and French of *câpe* and *cabouesse* are enclosed in parentheses,
as being, perhaps, West Indian. A " cob" is the offspring of black and mulatto
parents.

Creole.		English.		French.	
Masc.	Fem.	Masc.	Fem.	Masc	Fem.
carète	*cäouogne*	turtle		*caret*	
cousin	*cousine*	cousin			
dansèr	*dansèse*	dancer		*danseur*	*danseuse*
milâte	*milatresse*	mulatto	mulatress	*mulâtre*	*mulâtre*
nègue	*nègresse*	negro	negress	*nègre*	*négresse*

The following feminine forms are peculiar :—

Creole.		French.	English.
amise	*for*	*amie*	friend
bonbonnièse	„	*bonbonnière*	*Cr.* cake-woman
luvandèse	„	*lavandière*	laundress
léssivièse	*(from*	*lessiver)*	washer woman

CASE

Is the relation which a Noun bears to another Noun, a Verb, or a Preposition occurring in the same sentence.

We may allow three Cases in Creole; viz., the Nominative, Possessive, and Objective.

The Nominative is the Noun (or Pronoun) represented as *being* or *doing;* e.g : *toute* sêpent *cest sêpent,* every *snake* is a snake; *mauvés* mounes *ca vive longtemps,* wicked *people* live long.

In these sentences, *sêpent* and *mounes* are Nominatives, they being represented as being and doing respectively.

A Noun is Possessive when it designates the owner or possessor. In Creole the mode of forming this case is very simple. All that one has to do, is to name the possessor immediately *after* the object possessed; as, *caïe* Jean, *John's* house; *chapeau* papa *tit* fîe *la,* the *girl's father's* hat; i.e., (the) hat (of the) father (of the) girl This last rendering, which comes nearer to the Creole arrangement, is identical with the French construction, and shows that the former is a mere abbreviation of the latter; viz., (la) *case* (de) Jean; (le) *chapeau* (du) *père* (de la) *fille :*

Cr. *Bouöuique* missier la *té nans jâdin* Châles.
Fr. *Le bourrique* (de) l'homme *était dans (le) jardin* (de) *Charles.*
Eng. The donkey (of the) *man* was in (the) garden (of) Charles.

The Objective Case represents the Noun (or Pronoun) affected by
the action of a Verb, or governed by a Preposition; as,

> Cr.   *Misèr ca fair* macaques *manger* piment.
> Eng. Hard living makes *monkeys* eat *pepper.*
> Fr.   *La misère fait manger des* piments *aux* singes.
> Cr.   *Tout moune connaite* ça *qui ca bouïï nans* canari *yeaux.*
> Eng. Every body knows what is boiling in his earthen pot.
> Fr.   *Chacun sait ses affaires.*

Besides the above, we have in Creole a sort of Dative Case, denoting the individual to, for, or with regard to whom any thing is
done. The sign of this case is *ba* or *baï*, a shortening of the O. F. verb
bailler, to give; e.g: *li pôter tôuments* baï *famie 'i*, he brought trouble
to his relations; *li ca chaïer corps-li baï dents rie; lit.* he is convey-
ing himself *give* teeth to laugh; *i.e.*, he is exposing himself to
ridicule.

The two forms *ba* and *baï*, though identical in meaning, are not
indiscriminately used. *Ba* comes only before the Personal Pronouns, except *zôtes*, which perfers *baï;* e.g : ba *moèn;* ba *li; ba
yeaux.* In all other cases *baï* must be used; e.g : baï *yon madame;*
baï *fouèr moèn;* baï *ces mounes la : li câer fair gouös sauts* baï *zôtes,*
he will be defiant *towards* you.

ADJECTIVES.

An Adjective is a word which expresses the quality of a Noun;
as, *yon* grand *zaffair*, a *great* to-do; *yon* belle *fâce*, a *fine* joke.

Adjectives in Creole are any thing but well regulated. At every
turn we hear them used in French masculine forms to qualify feminine nouns, and *vice versâ.* But there is, nevertheless, a distinct,
though ill-sustained, attempt at gender inflection; especially in the
case of adjectives describing the qualities of *human* beings. As to
those that qualify nouns denoting animals and inanimate objects,
their forms depend on whether the nouns have been adopted from
the French by themselves, or so closely combined with the
adjectives as to convey a single, though composite idea. In the
former case, the adjective will have the form current in Creole : in
the latter, it will have the form required by French usage. For

example, *yon* grand *tâbe, plime* nêf, are the Creole equivalents of the
French *une* grande *table, plume* neuve, a *large* table, *new* pen. The
masculine forms *grand* and *néf* are employed in the Creole, because they
are the forms current in the dialect. But in *tâbe* ouönde, *round* table,
ouönde, (i.e. *ronde,)* the appropriate feminine adjective is used, because
it happens to be the form always employed in this particular connexion. Thus it is with all similar compounds borrowed bodily from
the French, and regarded in fact as a single word. In *chandelle*
ouömaine ; *toèle* grise ; grande *messe,* gouösse *pièce,* for example, the
adjectives *ouömaine, grise, grande, gouösse,* are femimine, in agreement
with the nouns combined with them, according to French practice ;
and it is so because each of these combinations conveys but a single
idea ; being, in fact, a mere appellation, like the English *broad-
cloth, hasty-pudding, sweet-meats,* &c.

With these general remarks, we proceed to minuter details.
First of all, we may dispose of adjectives ending in *e* mute, since
these, as in French, do not admit of any variation for gender ; e.g :
Fr. *un homme* fidèle, a *faithful* man, *une femme* fidèle, a *faithful* woman.
These adjectives have the same termination *(e)* in Creole, but those
in *le* drop *l, when it is preceded by a consonant;* as, Fr. *double, souple,
aimable,* etc., Cr. *doube, soupe, aimabe,* etc. But when a vowel comes
before *l,* it is retained ; as, Fr. *fragile, inutile,* Cr. *fouagile, initile.*
For the sake of sound, if *r* comes before the final *e,* the latter may
be dropped, as *r* is never heard in Creole at the end of words.

It has been stated above that there is some attempt at inflecting
Adjectives for Gender, especially when they denote the quality of
human beings. Of the Adjectives which are so inflected, the following are the most usual :—

a. Those ending in *és,* masc., *èse,* fem. Fr. *ais, aise ;* e.g :

Creole.	*English.*	*French*
anglés, anglèse	English	*anglais, anglaise*
fouancés, fouancèse	French	*français, française*

But *pótiaés, écossés, ilandés,* etc. are not usually inflected in Creole.

b. Adjectives ending in *r,* masc., *se,* fem. ; e.g :

ouachèr, ouachèse	foppish, ostentatious	
escandalèr, escandulèse	noisy	

Creole.	English.	French.
flattèr, flattèse	*Cr.* sycophantic	*flatteur, flatteuse*

c. Adjectives ending in *in*, masc., *ine*, fem. ; e.g :

Creole.	English.	French.
cochin, cochine	roguish	*coquin, coquine*
malin, maline	cunning	*malin, maligne*

d. Adjectives ending in *x*, masc., *se*, fem. ; e.g :

Creole.	English.	French.
jaloux, jalouse	jealous	
malhéréx, malhèrèse	*Cr.* indigent, very poor	*malheureux, euse*
vertouéx, ve, touèse	virtuous	*vertueux, euse*

The French masculine form seems to be preferred in the case of adjectives terminating in *nt*, *is*, *t*, which two last are mostly participial. In French an *e* mute is added to these endings to form the feminine.

Examples of adjectives in *nt*, *is*, and *it*, uninflected :—

Cr. *Yon viécorps qui* hampant.
Eng. An old man who is grasping.
Fr. *Un vieillard qui est avare.*

Cr. *Mamzelle la assez* insolent *poû lot li.*
Eng. That (young) lady has her full share of insolence.
Fr. *Cette demoiselle est assez* insolente *pour sa part.*

Cr. *Missier la sembe con si li té bien* soupouis ; *et madame li té* soupouis *tou.*
Eng. The gentleman seems to have been greatly *surprised* ; and his wife was *surprised* also.
Fr. *Ce monsieur parait avoir été très* surpris : *et sa femme (était* surprise) *aussi.*

Cr. *Ce tits fies la té bien* distréts *nans lapouièrs yeaux.*
Eng. The girls were greatly *distracted* in their prayers.
Fr. *Ces enfants étaient très* distraites *dans leurs prières.*

Cr. *Yon nômme* instouit ; *yon femme* instouit.
Eng. A *well-taught* man ; a *well-taught* woman.
Fr. *Un homme* instruit ; *une femme* instruite.

The following adjectives are usually employed in the masculine form alone :—

Creole.	English.	French.	
Masc. & Fem.		Masc.	Fem.
blanc	white	*blanc*	*blanche*
épés	thick	*épais*	*épaisse*

Creole.	English.	French.	
Masc. & Fem.		**Masc.**	**Fem.**
faux	false	*faux*	*fausse*
fin	fine	*fin*	*fine*
fort	strong	*fort*	*forte*
foués	fresh, cool	*frais*	*fraiche*
gaucher	left-handed, awkward	*gaucher*	*gauchère*
gouös	big, coarse	*gros*	*grosse*
grand	large	*grand*	*grande*
gras	fat	*gras*	*grasse*
gris	grey	*gris*	*grise*
jimeau	twin	*jumeau*	*jumelle*
loûd	heavy	*lourd*	*lourde*
pitit, 'tit	little, small	*petit*	*petite*
sain	wholesome	*sain*	*saine*
sec	dry, crisp, curt	*sec*	*seche*

The following are used in the French feminine form only :

Creole.	English.	French.	
adoète	adroit	*adroit*	*adroite*
belle	beautiful	*beau*	*belle*
chèce	dry (not wet)	*sec*	*seche*
coûte	short	*court*	*courte*
doète	straight	*droit*	*droite*
étoète	narrow	*étroit*	*étroite*
fine	Cr. slender	*fin*	*fine*
foète	cold	*froid*	*froide*
laide	ugly	*laid*	*laide*
lasse	weary	*las*	*lasse*
légèr	light	*léger*	*légère*
lente	slow	*lent*	*lente*
longue	long	*long*	*longue*
miette, mouette	dumb, silent	*muet*	*muette*
molle	soft	*mou*	*molle*
naïvé	Cr. candid	*naïf*	*naïve*
nette	clean	*net*	*nétte*
sotte	silly	*sot*	*sotte*
soûde	deaf, dull	*sourd*	*sourde*
toute	all	*tout*	*toute*

The following are peculiar in formation or with regard to origin :—

Creole.	English.	French Etymology.
blêmisse	palish	*(blême)*
bouïèl	brilliant, lively	*(briller)*
ealeau	hard-up	
came-came	brazen	
chacal	stingy, shabby	
congosal	litigious, quarrelsome	
couyasse	foolish, silly	
dènde	determined	
doubadou, dibadi	dandified	*(troubadour)*
foubèn, foubien	reckless	
foutèse	small, paltry	
fouti	ruined, " done for"	*(fichu)*
GènGènfouñan GanGanfouñan }	showy	
gouosièse, f	coarse mannered	*(grossière)*
hampant	grasping, avaricious	*(happer)*
jolotte	lovely	*(joli)*
macan·la	foppish, ostentatious	
mélouèr, èse	meddlesome	*(mèler)*
ñeñèn, ïen-ïèn	whimpering, fond of crying	
ouachèr, se	showy, dressy	
piôcô (Sp. *poco,*)	paltry, small	
ranCHinèse, f	implacable, malice-bearing	*(rancunière)*
wawà	woe-begone	
wangané, wanganèn	addicted to sorcery	

DEGREES OF COMPARISON.

There are three Degrees of Comparison :—

a. The Positive, or the Adjective itself; e.g: *mélouèr,* meddlesome ; *ououlant,* cunning.

b. The Comparative, which is formed by prefixing *plis,* Fr. *plus,* more, (and sometimes *moèns* or *moènce,*) to the Adjective: thus, *plis mélouèr,* more meddlesome ; *moènce ououlant,* less cunning.

c. The Superlative. This is expressed in the same way as the Comparative, and must be gathered from the context. In proverbial and other phrases from the French, the Superlative is, of course, according to French custom; e.g :

> Cr. Plis grand *macanda moèn jamain voèr.*
> Eng. The *greatest* muff I ever saw.
> Fr. *Le plus grand fat que j'aie jamais vu*
> Cr. La plis belle *en-bas la baîe,* lit. the prettiest (is) under the tub. *As a proverb :*—the best is yet to come.
> Fr. La plus belle *est sous la baille.*

Sometimes the Superlative is expressed by means of a relative phrase containing the Comparative, with the words *passé toute* added ; e.g : *ça qui plis jolette* passé toute *la,* that which is the *prettiest* of all.

IRREGULAR COMPARATIVES.

The Creole cannot be said to have Comparatives that are irregular, at least in the sense in which the following are so in French :—

	French.		*Creole.*
Pos.	Comp.	Pos.	Comp.
bon, good	*meilleur,* better	*bon*	*mèièr, plis bon*
mauvais, bad	*pïre,** worse	*mauvés*	*plus mauvés*
petit, small	*moindre,* smaller	*pitit*	*plis pitit*

COMPARISONS.

Comparisons of Superiority are made in Creole, *(a)* by placing *plis* before the Adjective and *passé* after it; and *(b)* by means of *passé* alone; e.g : *zorèies pas doé* plis *hauts* passé *téte,* the ears should not be *higher* than the head, Fr. *les oreilles ne doivent pas étre* plus *haut placées* que *la téte; viècorps cela-la ca coèr li bon* passé *toute moune,* this old man believes himself *better* than every body, Fr. *ce vieillard se croit* meilleur *que tout le monde; ous grand* passé *li,* you are *bigger* than he, Fr. *vous étes plus grand* que *lui.*

Equality is sometimes denoted by placing *aussi* before the Adjective and *qui,* Fr. *que,* after it: thus—*Gangane yeaux* aussi *viéx* qui *mounonque nous,* their grandmother (is) *as* old *as* our uncle, Fr. *leur grand'mère est* aussi *vieille* que *nôtre oncle.*

---

* Sometimes *plus mauvais.*—DELILLE.

But oftener the Adjective has only *con*, Fr. *comme*, after it; e.g: *caïe Jean néf* con *cela Vitor*, John's house (is as) new *as* Victor's, Fr. *la maison de Jean est* aussi *neuve* que *celle de Victor*.

Inferiority is expressed:—

a. By negativing the Comparative of Equality; as, *ous* pas *bon con li*, you are *not* (as) good as he, Fr. *vous n'êtes* pas *aussi bon que lui*; *yon matapèl* pas *faibe con yon manicou*, an ant-eater is *not so* weak as an opossum.

b. By placing *moènce*, Fr. *moins*, before the Adjective and *qui* (sometimes *passé*,) after it; e.g: *yon drivaïèr* moènce *sèvïabe* qui (or *passé*) *yon moune qui ca réter lacaie*, a rover is of *less* service *than* a person who stays at home, Fr. *un vagabond est* moins *serviable* qu' *une personne qui se tient chez lui*.

The Superlative Absolute is expressed by placing *bien*, *touöp*, (Fr. *trop*) or *tout*, before the Adjective; e.g: *ah, moncher ça té* bien *bon*, ah, my friend, that was *very* good, Fr. *ah, moncher c'était* bien *bon.*; *blow çala* touöp *belle*, this affair is *exceedingly* fine, Fr. *cette affaire est* trop *jolie; tit mammaïe la* tout *jolotte*, that little child is *very* lovely, Fr. *Cet enfant est* très-*joli*.

Sometimes a repitition of the Adjective serves the same purpose; as, *yeaux chémber yon* gouös, gouös *caïman*, they (have) caught a *very* large crocodile, Fr. *ils ont pris un* très-*gros crocodile*.

Another mode, which is now almost out of fashion, (being confined to a few old persons in country districts,) is to place *tout-plein*, (all full) after the Adjectives:—*malongue moèn goûmand* tout plein, my shipmate is *very* close-fisted.

ADJECTIVES—NUMERALS.

The Numerals Adjectives are, with a few exceptions, pronounced as in French. The differences are as follow:

CARDINAL NUMBERS.

Creole.	English.	French.
yone	one	*un, une*
déx	two	*deux*
tois	three	*trois*
quâte	four	*quâtre*

These Creole forms are preserved in all cases.

The *q* in *cinq*, five, is sounded in French when the word is alone, or comes before a vowel sound; but in Creole the same pronunciation, i.e. *senk*, is always adhered to;* e.g :

cinq entétés (scnk-an-tay-tay)	five obstinates	*cinq entêtés*
cinq joûs (senk-zhoo)	five days	*cinq jours*

With regard to *six* and *dix* (six and ten) there is some inconsistency. We say *six goûdes* (see good), six dollars, *dix doégts* (dee dway) ten fingers, etc., in strict accordance with French custom, which makes the *x* silent before consonants. But, strangely enough, we also say *six misiciens* (seece mc-ze-se-enh), six musicians, *dix batimens* (deece bah-te-manh), ten vessels; besides sounding *x* in hundred other instances before consonants.

FRACTIONAL NUMBERS.

Creole.	*English.*	*French.*
dimi, motiz	half	*demi, demie, moitié*
yon tiers	the third	*le tiers*
tois quâts	three-quarters	*les trois quarts*

The Creole seldom go farther than the above fractional parts.

PROPORTIONALS.

The only proportionals we have heard used are :—.

doûbe	double	*le double.*
tribs.	triple	*le triple*

PRONOUNS.

A Pronoun is a word used instead of a Noun; e.g : *hier, mcèz et-pts sésé ous té si pèr*, nous *pouend cououi*, yesterday, *I* and *your* sister were so frightened, (that) *we* took to our heels, Fr. *hier*, votro *sœur et moi*, nous *avions une si grand' peur, que nous prîmes la fuite; hamac la té plis haut, main* zòtes *bésser* li, the hammock was higher up, but *you* lowered *it*, Fr. *le hamac était plus haut, mais* vous *l'avez baissé.*

---

* *Cinq-sous* (senh-soo), five cents, presents an exception; but the compound is regarded as a single word, involving but little, if any, reference to the component values of the coin.

There are seven kinds of Pronouns that we will notice; viz., Personal, Possessive, Relative, Demonstrative, Indefinite, Reflexive, and Interrogative.

PERSONAL PRONOUNS

Stand for the names of individuals. In Creole they are as follow :—

	SINGULAR.				PLURAL.	
Cr.	Eng.	Fr.		Cr.	Eng.	Fr.
1. *moèn*	I	*moi (je)*	1.	*Nous*	we	*nous*
2. *ous*	you	*vous (tu)*	2.	*zôtcs*	ye, you	*vous (autres)*
3. *li, 'i*	he, she, it	*il elle*	3.	*yeaux,*	they	*ils, elles (eux)*

These Pronouns are sometimes called Conjunctives, because they are used in conjunction with Verbs; thus :—*moncher*, moèn *ca páler, et-pis cest poú* ous *couter : si* yeaux *aller nans tou crabe, faut* zôtes *poñèn* yeaux, my friend, *I* speak, and *you* are to hearken : if *they* enter a crab's hole, *you* must catch them.

FORMATION OF THE PERSONAL PRONOUNS.

To persons acquainted with French, nothing can be more obvious than the origination of the Creole Pronouns. But to those of our readers who may not know French, the following explanations may possess some interest :—

Moèn, which represents the French *moi*, has been modified by the usual change of *oi* into *oè*, and the further addition of *n*. There can be no doubt that the fuller sound of *moi*, together with its frequency in familiar discourse, led to its adoption in preference to *je*, the proper Nominative.

Tu, the second person singular of the French Personals, has had, in the Trinidadian dialect, a singular fate. After diligent search, we discovered it at the tail of two words; the one an *adverb*, and the other an *interrogative particle*, itself perverted and bereft of half its primeval force. The adverb in question is *óti*, (where,) and the particle, *péli*, (can?). Were it not for the fulness of our conviction on the point, we should have hesitated to give the question *où es-tu ?* where *art thou,* as the etymology of *óti*, where. But, after all, there are stranger things in the Science of Language; and, upon reflection, we are disposed to retract the apology introducing a derivation which is, on the whole, so obvious.

The Creoles, to ask a question in which the possibility of one's doing a thing is involved, employ *péti* as auxilliary to the principal Verb :—thus, *zôtes* péti *coèr papa moèn die yon baggaie con ça?* can you (possibly) believe that my father said such a thing? That the French *peux-tu*, canst thou, is the original of *péti*, is a fact admitting of no dispute. In some of the other Islands, *tu* has enjoyed better fortune. The forms *to*, Nominative, and *toé*, Possessive (and sometimes Objective), are honoured by elderly folk in Martinique, Guadaloupe, etc. ; but to *us*, the sound of these words is very tickling. *Si* to *badnèn épis* cnèmbois, *papa* tcé '*a bicher* toé, is the Guadaloupian way of saying: *si* ous *badnèn épis* (or *àvec*) *sôcier*, *papa* ous *va batte* ous, if *you* dabble in sorcery, *your* father will beat *you.* We, however, hear *to* and *toé* in *bellairs* composed in country districts here ; but the use of them is generally satirical.

With regard to *li*, which the Creoles sometimes shorten into '*i*, it is a corruption of *le*, the French third person masculine Accusative.

Zôtes is formed on the same principle with *zassiette, zepingue,** etc. The frequent hearing of the colloquial *vous autres* from their owners, gave rise to the formation of this word by the Negroes.

In *yeaux*, which is clearly *eux*, the initial *y* is but a fulcrum for the voice.†

POSSESSIVE PRONOUNS.*

Possessive Pronouns stand for the name of the owner or possessor. They are of two kinds ; viz : Conjunctive and Disjunctive.

a. Conjunctive Possessives are employed always in conjunction with the Noun possessed. In Creole the Personal Pronouns become Possessives of this class by being merely added to the Noun ; e.g:

SINGULAR.

Creole.	English.	French.
1. *bohôtés* moèn	1. *my* effects	1. *mes effets*

---

* See page 17.

† Compare, for instance, the first syllable of the Spanish *yerro* with *err* in Lat. *erro*, and that of the Indian word *yankee* or *yengee* with *eng(l)* in the word *English.* For further remarks on the Pronouns, see Syntax.

Creole.	English.	French.
2. *gogo* ous	2. *your* namesake	2. *ton (votre) homonyme*
3. *sottises* li	3. *his, her* abuse	3. *ses injures*

PLURAL.

Creole.	English.	French.
1. *bitation* nous	1. *our* estate	1. *notre habitation*
2. *horrôpe* zôtes	2. *your* scrape	2. *votre embarras*
3. *zancêles* yeaux	3. *their* forefathers	3. leurs *ancêtres*

b. Disjunctive Possessives come always by themselves. These in Creole are composed of the Demonstrative *cela*, (slah,) that, prefixed to the Personals; e.g:

SINGULAR.

Creole.	English.	French.
1. *cela-moèn*	1. mine	1. *le* mien, *la* miènne etc.
2. *cela-ous*	2. yours	2. *le* tien, *la* tienne, etc.
3. *cela-li, cela-ï*	3. his hers, its	3. *le* sien, *la* sienne, etc.

PLURAL.

Creole.	English.	French.
1. *cela-nous*	1. ours	1. *le, la* nôtre, *les* nôtres
2. *cela-zôtes*	2. yours	2. *le, la* vôtre, *les* vôtres
3. *cela-yeaux*	3. theirs	3. *le, la* leur, *les* leurs.

ILLUSTRATIONS.

Cr. *Macaque dîe ça qui nans bouche li pas* cela-li.
Eng. Monkey has said (that) what's in his mouth is not *his*.
Fr. *Le singe a dit que ce qui est dans sa bouche n'est pas à lui*.
Cr. *Cela qui moune live la yest? Cest* cela-nous.
Eng. Whose is the book? It is *ours*.
Fr. *A qui est le livre? C'est* le nôtre.
Cr. *Oti* cela-zôtes? *Li tomber nans pît èvec* cela-yeaux.
Eng. Where (is) *yours?* It fell in (the) well (along) with *theirs*.
Fr. *Où est* le vôtre? *Il est tombe dans (le) puit avec* le leur.

REMARKS.

Natives of Guadaloupe, etc. form those Possessives somewhat differently; e.g:

a. Conjunctives :—

Creole	English	French
1. *pays* à-*moèn*	1. my countryman	1. *mon compatriote*
2. *bitin* à-*ous*	2. your (portable) property	2. *vos baggages*
3. *pôpôte* à-*li*	3. her doll	3. *sa poupee*

b. Disjunctives :—

Creole.	English.	French.
1. *ta moèn*	1· mine	1. *le mien,* etc.
2. *ta toé*	2. thine, yours	2. *le tien,* etc.
3. *ta li*	3. his, hers, its	3. *le sien,* etc.

This is a mutilation of the French Possessive construction, *être -à*; e.g: *c'est à moi,* it is *mine,* etc.

RELATIVE PRONOUNS

Are so called because they relate to some Noun or Pronoun preceding them.

We employ but two Relatives in the Trinidadian Patois : viz., *qui,* who, which; and *ça,* whom, which. The following are illustrations of their use :

(qui)

Cr. *Toèle la* qui *la-sous lingue* la.*
Eng. The cloth *which* is on the line.
Fr. *La toile* qui *est sur la ligne.*

(ça)

Cr. *Chapeau la* ça *papa moèn pêde la.*
Eng. The hat *which* my father lost.
Fr. *Le chapeau* que *mon père a perdu.*
Cr. *Missier la* ça *yeaux pougaller la.*
Eng. The man *whom* they thrust out.
Fr. *Le monsieur* qu'on a mis *dehors.*

Except by children, *ça* is, however, seldom thus employed. The most ordinary mode of expressing objective relations of this sort, is by omitting the pronoun altogether, as is usually done in familiar English, when, for example, we say : *the hat my father bought for me, the man they thrust out,* the relative *which* being omitted in the first sentence, and *whom* in the second. In Creole these phrases are ordinarily : *chapeau la papa moèn gañèn ba moèn la; missier la yeaux pougaller la.*

HE WHO, THEY WHO, (Fr. *celui qui—ceux qui*) are represented in Creole by *ça qui;* e.g : ça qui *content bébelle doé travale poú li, they who* like finery ought to work for it, Fr. ceux qui *aiment des ornements doivent travailler pour les avoir.*

* Pronounced *leeng.*

WHAT, the Compound Relative, Fr. *ce que, ce dont,* etc. is like-wise *ça* in Creole; e.g :—

Cr. *Ous trapper ça ous té envie 'a.*
Eng. You have got *what* you desired.
Fr. *Vous avez obtenu* ce que *vous désiriéz.*
Cr. *Moèn pas voèr* ça *ous té pâler moèn la.*
Eng. I have not seen *that* of *which* you had spoken to me.
Fr. *Je n'ai pas vu* ce dont *vous aviez parlé.*

DEMONSTRATIVE PRONOUNS

Serve to point out objects. In Creole there is, strictly speaking, but *one* Demonstrative Pronoun; viz: *cela-la (slah-lah,)* or *ça-la,* and this, like the Article Definite, always comes *after* its Noun; e.g:

Cr. *Zombi* cela-la; Eng. *this* ghost Fr. cette *apparition.*
Cr. *Jipe* çala; Eng. *this* skirt; Fr. cette *jupe.*

THESE, the plural of THIS, is expressed in Creole by placing *ces* before the Substantive and *cela-là (slah*-lah) or *ça-la* after it; e.g: *toutes* ces *coupons* cela-là *pas lâges,* all *these* (cloth) remnants are not wide, Fr. *tous* ces *coupons ne sont pas larges;* ces *baggaïes* ça-là *pas ca fair moèn plésir, these* things do not please me, Fr. ces *choses ne me plaisent pas.*

The Demonstrative, THAT, which serves to point out remote objects, has no exact equivalent in Creole. Sometimes, and especially in relative clauses, and after Possessives, the Creole Definite Article *(la)* resumes its demonstrative import; e.g :—

Cr. *Nômme* la *ous té ouèr là-bas-là.*
Eng. *That* man whom you saw yonder.
Fr. Cet *homme que vous avez vu là-bas.*
Cr. *Jadin* moén la *couvert épîs zêbes*
Eng. *That* garden of mine is overgrown with grass.
Fr. *Mon jardin est rempli d'herbes.*

Ces has already been noticed as performing in Creole the function of Plural Definite Article. The same construction with *la* is used to express the Plural Demonstrative, THOSE; e.g : *oui,* ces *joûs* la *té bons joûs,* yes, *those* days were good days, Fr. *oui,* ces *jours-là étaient de bons jours.*

INDEFINITE PRONOUNS, &c.

To a certain class of words bearing a vague pronominal import, Grammarians have given the name of Indefinite Pronouns. Some of these are adjectives, and are sometimes joined to Nouns, while others are substantives or abbreviated phrases.

The following are the most usual in Creole :—

Creole.	*English.*	*French.*
aïen, aïlen	nothing	*rien*
aucHaine	no, adj.	*aucun, aucune*
ça	whatever	*ce que*
chaque	each, every	
chaquin	every one	*chaqu'un, une*
cHécHin	some one	*quelqu'un, une*
cHêque	some	*quelque*
cHêque-moune	somebody	*quelqu'un, une*
cHêque-zins	some, a few	*quelques-uns, unes*
dôte	other, some other	*d'autres*
en-pile, yon pile	many	*beaucoup (de gens)*
lézôtes	others	*autrui, les autres*
lôte	the other	*l'autre*
moune	people, they, one	*on*
ni yone ni lôte	neither; both	*ni l'un ni l'autre*
pêsonne	no one, nobody	*pergonne*
qui-ci-soit	any—soever	*qui ce soit*
tel moune	such a one	*un tel*
tous-lé-déx	both	*l'un et l'autre*
toute-baggaïe	everything	*tout, toute*
toute ça	everything, whatever	*tout ce (que)*
toute-moune	everybody	*tout le monde*
yeaux	people, folk	*on*
yon moune	a body, some one	*quelqu'un*
yone et-lôte, yone-à-lôte	one another	*l'un et l'autre*
yone-o-bèn-lôte, yone-o-lôte	either, one or the other	*l'un ou l'autré*
yon tel	such a one	*un tel*

ILLUSTRATIONS.

Cr. Yon moune *die moèn li ouèr nous.*

Eng. *Some one* told me he saw us.

Fr. Quelqu'un *m'a dit nous avoir vus.*

ILLUSTRATIONS.

Cr. *Pas fair* lézôtcs *ça ous pas sé vlé ycaux fair zôtés.*
Eng. Do not to *others* what you would not wish them do to you.
Fr. Ne *faites pas* à autrui *ce que vous ne voudriez pas qu'on vous fît.*

Cr. Ycaux ca *die yon pile baggaïes conte le.*
Eng. *People* say many things against him.
Fr. On *dit beaucoup de choses contre lui.*

Cr. *Pouend* ça *yeaux ba ous.*
Eng. Take *whatever* they give you.
Fr. *Prenez* ce qu'*on vous donne.*

Cr. Moune ca coñèn *nans lapôte la.*
Eug. *Some one* is knocking at the door.
Fr. On *frappe à la porte.*

Cr. Chaquin *ca chonger ôni poû corp-yeaux.*
Eng. *Each* is thinking only of himself.
Fr. Chaqu'un *ne pense qu'à soi.*

Cr. *Si* yeaux *té die* tel mounc *té ca châcher nous.*
Eng. If *they* had said *such a one* had been seeking us.
Fr. *Si* l'on *avait dit* qu'un tel *nous cherchait.*

Cr. *Moèn pas ca doe* ni yone ni lôtc.
Eng. I owe *neither* (of them).
Fr. *Je ne dois ni* à l'un *ni* à l'autre.

Cr. *Tit fic la jirer* ni yone ni lôte.
Eng. The girl abused them *both.*
Fr. *La fille invectiva* l'un et l'autre.

Cr. *Oti fouèr moèn yest là, li foubèn* toute-baggaïe.
Eng. In his present condition, my brother is regardless of *every thing.*
Fr. *Dans l'état où mon frère se trouve, il ne regardé* rien.

Cr. Pêsonne *pas jamain die ça.*
Eng. *No one* ever said that.
Fr. Personne *n'a dit cela.*

REFLEXIVE PRONOUNS.

A Reflexive Pronoun represents at the same time the agent and object of an action. In Creole, the noun *corps*, body, prefixed to the Personals, expresses the reflexive idea in a manner at once natural and forcible :—

	Creole.	English.	French.
		SINGULAR.	
1.	*corps-moèn*	myself	*me*
2.	*corps-ous*	yourself	*te, vous*
3.	*corps-li*	himself, herself, itself	*ε*
		PLURAL.	
1.	*corps-nous*	ourselves	*nous*
2.	*corps-zôtes*	yourselves	*vous*
3.	*corps-yeaux*	themselves	*se*

ILLUSTRATIONS.

Cr. *Moèn té ca pâler baï* corps-moèn.
Eng. I was speaking to *myself*.
Fr. *Je parlais à* moi-même

Cr. *Ous c'aller fini èvec* corps-ous.
Eng. You will ruin *yourself*.
Fr. *Vous allez vous perdre.*

Cr. *Capitaine la blesser* corps-li.
Eng. The captain wounded *himself*.
Fr. *Le capitaine s'est blessé.*

Cr. *Anouns chapper* corps-nous.
Eng. Let us take *ourselves* off.
Fr. *Echappons nous.*

Cr. *Zôtes pas connaîte* corps-zôtes.
Eng. You don't know *your (own) selves.*
Fr. *Vous ne vous connaissez pas.*

Cr. *Yeaux amboèse* corps-yeaux.
Eng. They (hurriedly) concealed *themselves.*
Fr. *Ils se sont (vitement) cachés.*

When SELF is merely emphatic, it is rendered, as in French, by adding *même* ; e.g :—

1.	*moèn-même*	myself	*moi-même*
2.	*ous-même*	yourself	*vous-même*
3.	*li-même, 'i-même*	himself, herself, itself	*lui-même*

	Creole.	*English.*	*French.*
1.	*nous-mêmes*	ourselves	*nous-mêmés*
2.	*zôtes-mêmes*	yourselves	*vous-mêmes*
3.	*yeaux-mêmes*	themselves	*eux-mêmes*

Cr. *Moèn pè ouèr* ça moèn-même, I can see that *myself,* Fr. *Je puis voir cela* moi-même.

Cr. *Fair toute travaîe la* ous-même, do all the work *yourself,* Fr. *faites tout le travail* vous-même.

Cr. *Missier la happer tit mamaie la* li-même, the gentleman **himself** seized the child, Fr. *le monsieur a saisi l'enfant* lui-même.

Very often, for the sake of greater emphasis, the Reflexives and Compound Personals are combined ; as,

Cr. *Ous ca badinèn* corps-ous-même, you are deceiving *your (own)* self, Fr. *vous vous trompez* vous-même.

INTERROGATIVE PRONOUNS

Serve to ask questions. Those commonly employed in Creole are :—

à qui? who ? whose ? *ça ?* (before relatives) who ? what ? *qui?* what ? *qui ça ?* what ? *quil-estce?* which ? which of them ? *qui-moune?* who ?

ILLUSTRATIONS.

Cr. à qui *ous?* *who* are you ? Fr. qui *êtes-vous?*

Cr. ça qui *là ?* *who (what)* is there ? Fr. qui *est-là ?*

Cr. ça *ous pêle?* *what* (have) you lost ? Fr. qu'*avez-vous perdu?*

Cr. *compte* qui moune *zôtes ca pâler ?* of *whom* are you speaking ? Fr. *de* qui *parlez-vous ?*

Cr. qui! *marron?* *what!* run away ? Fr. quoi! *évader ?*

Cr. *main,* qui ça *ous baîe?* but, *what* did you give ? Fr. *mais,* qu'*avez-vous donné?*

Cr. quil-estce *ous simiér?* *which* do you prefer ? Fr. lequel *préférez-vous ?*

Cr. qui-moune ça *ca vinî là ? who* is it coming there ? Fr. qui *est celui qui vient là ?*

VERBS.

A Verb is a word which denotes being or doing.

With some few exceptions, the Verbs in Creole are French Infinitives, often altered by mispronunciation. In adopting this part of speech, the original framers of the dialect, having no other guide than the ear, not seldom made Infinitives of past participles, indi-catives, imperatives, and, sometimes, of even nouns, adjectives and other parts of speech. In a set of Verbs so irregularly de-rived, we should look in vain for that uniformity of ending, which prevails in the French Conjugations. Nevertheless, a clear insight into this part of Creole Grammar may be obtained, if, setting aside the question of form, we examine the Verbs only with reference to their actual derivation. Thus considered, they fall under *five* heads, according as they represent, *(a)* real French Infinitives; *(b)* Past Participles; *(c)* Indicatives; *(d)* Imperatives; and *(e)* Nouns, Adjectives, etc. converted into verbs.

a.   FRENCH INFINITIVES.

1.   Most verbs ending in the sound of *é(r)* ; as,

Creole.	*English.*	*French.*
blâmer	to blame	*blâmer*
crier	to call ; Cr. to name	
fiñoler, fiñonler	to flourish *(trans.)*	*fignoler*
gônâder	to deride, to provoke	*goguenarder*
sauter	to leap, jump	
*simèn**	to scatter abroad	*semer*
touver	to find	*trouver*
vider	to pour out	

2.   Verbs having the final sound of *i*, which represents *ir* of the second French Conjugation :—

accompli	Cr. to fulfil	*accomplir*
banni	to banish	*bannir*
cououî	to run	*courir*
fouémi, fouèmî	to shudder	*frémir*
gâni	to garnish	*garnir*
haï	to hate	*haïr*
vêti	to warn	*avertir*

3.   The following verbs of the third French Conjugation in *voir*, Cr. *voèr* :—

avoèr	Cr. to procure, (to have)	*avoir*, to have

* As has been remarked at page 5, the terminational *er* is usually converted into *en*, after a nasal. This change affects very many infinitives of the first French Conjugation ; e.g : *bimèn, ycûnèn, simèn, toûnen*, etc., for *abimer, (se) gourmer, semer, tourner*, etc.

Creole.	English.	French.
apêcivoèr, pêcivoèr	to perceive	apercevoir
récivoèr, ricivoèr, riçouvoèr	to receive	recevoir
rivoèr*	to see again, to ask again	revoir, to see again
voèr, ouèr	to see	voir

4. Infinitives of the fourth French Conjugation, sounded in Creole without the *r* :—

confie	to comfit, boil in sugar	confire
coude	to sew	coudre
fouie	to fry	frire
vive	to live	vivre

But when *re* is in French preceded by *nd* (i.e. *ndre*), both *d* and *r* are dropped :—

craine	to fear	craindre
fône	to melt	fondre
joène	to join	joindre
répône	to answer	repondre

NOTE.—To avoid too wide a departure from the French orthography, we have retained *d*, when *n* before it is preceded by *e*; as dropping the former letter totally changes the pronunciation. The *d*, however, must not be sounded :—

attende (attann)	to wait for	attendre
fende (fann)	to split	fendre
vende (vann)	to sell	vendre

b. FRENCH PAST PARTICIPLES BECOME INFINITIVES † IN CREOLE.

apêcî	to perceive, i.e.	aperçu	past par. of			apercevoir
assiss	to sit	„	assise, f	„	„ „	s'asseoir
commis	to commit	„	commis	„	„ „	commettre
couvèr	to cover	„	couvert	„	„ „	couvrir
dèmis, démis	to sprain	„	demis	„	„ „	demettre
échi	to elapse	„	échu	„	„ „	échoir

* This verb is often used in the latter sense—as, *ous pas tni aïen à rivoèr épis moèn*, you have nothing *more to ask* (or to *seek*) from me.

† For examples of this kind of verb-derivation, compare the English to *accrue*, to *apprise*, from *accrû*, past part. of *accroîte*, and *appris*, past part. of *apprendre*, and verbs ending in *ate*, from *Lat.* past parts. in *atus*.

Creole.	*English.*			*French.*			
môr	to die	i.e.	*mort*	past. part. of			*mourir*
né	to be born	„	*né*	„	„	„	*naître*
ouvèr	to open	„	*ouvert*	„	„	„	*ouvrir*
pêdi	to lose	„	*perdu*	„	„	„	*perdre*
résoli	to resolve	„	*resolu*	„	„	„	*résoudre*
souffèr	to suffer	„	*souffert*	„	„	„	*souffrir*

Souffoui (for *souffrir*) is pretty often heard in our Patois; but *couvoui, mououi, ouvoui* (for *couvrir, mourir, ouvrir*), are used only by natives of Guadaloupe, Martinique, etc.

c.　　　　　　　INDICATIVE CONVERSIONS.

The following verbs are conversions of French Indicatives into Infinitives. It being difficult, in most of these cases, to determine what particular person of a given tense may have been at first adopted, we deem it best to do away with inflectional forms in this section also, when that could be effected without altering the sound. For instance, we give the artificial form *vaû*, instead of *vaux* or *vaut*, both of which are pronounced *vo*.* The other substitutions, with their probable originals, may be seen in the subjoined list :—

baîe	to give	from	*baille, baillent*	Ind. Pres. of *bailler*
doë	to owe		*dois, doit (devez?)*	„ ﾟ„　„ *devoir*
môde	to bite, (of a fish)		*mordent (mordre?)*	„ „　„ *mordre*
pé	to be able		*peux, peut*	„ „　„ *pouvoir*
sa	to be able }		*savent*	„ „　„ *savoir*
save	to know }			
té	was		*étais, était*	„ Imp.　„ *être*
travaîe	to work		*travaille, travaillent*	„ Pres.　„ *travailler*
vaû	to be worth		*vaux, vaut*	„ „　„ *valoir*
vlé	to want		*voulez (voulais, voulait?)*	„　„etc.„ *vouloir*

To these may be added *voudré* and *sé*, which represent the French conditionals *voudrais* (or *voudrait*), and *serais* (or *serait)*; and finally, *ensouhaite*, which forms a sort of optative.

d.　　　　　　　VERBS FROM THE IMPERATIVE.

We give the following as derived from Imperatives, although they may, with a single exception, be from the second person plural

* See Orthography, page 12.

Indicative Present as well.   But, for reasons hereafter to be
stated,* we think the presumption is in favour of the former view.
The matter, however, is of small consequence. In the following
list, the verbs in *ez* are spelt with an *er*, to secure a distinction
between actual and derivational Infinitives.

Creole.	*English.*	*French*
môder, moder	to bite	i.e. *mordez* 2 pl. Imper. of *mordre*
défaite	to loose	„ *defaites* „ „ „ „ *défaire*
métter	to put on, wear	„ *mettez* „ „ „ „ *mettre*
soucourer	to aid	„ *secourez* „ „ „ „ *secourir*
tienne	to hold, keep	„ (*qu'il*) *tienne* 3 sing. „ *tenir*

c.   NOUNS AND ADJECTIVES EMPLOYED AS VERBS.

bisoèn	to need	from *avoir besoin (de)*
content	to like	„ *être content (de)*
crēdî	to give or take credit	„ *vendre ou acheter à crédit*
envie	to long for, to desire	„ *avoir envie (de)*
gāouler	to romp	„ *garruleux* (adj.)
jaloû	to envy, be jealous of	„ *être jaloux (de)*
mecontent	to grow dissatisfied with	„ *être mécontent (de)*
pèx	to be silent	„ *paix !*
pèr	to fear, to dread	„ *avoir peur (de)*
plein	to fill	„ *plein* (adj.)
soèn	to care, to nurse	„ *avoir soin (de)*
soucier, pas sou-cier	to care nothing for	„ *être soucieux, to be anxious*

To these may be added *acoupi*, to stoop or squat; *ageounoux*, to
kneel, Fr. *croupir; être à genoux.*

VERBS PECULIAR TO THE CREOLE.

In conformity with our plan, we here present a few specimens
of verbs peculiar as to origin or formation, with one or two
from English and Spanish :—

amagoter	to bind, wrap up	(*magot*)
amblouser	to deceive	
aouantar	to contend	(Sp. *aguantar*)

* See Syntax of the Personal Pronouns.

Creole.	*English.*	*Etymology.*
bobo	to hurt, annoy	
boucanèn, boucaner	to smoke *(trans)*.	
bouffeter	to snub	
cancansiner	to stagnate	(calciner?)
cнêmbér*	to hold, seize	(tiens bien?)
chèper	to excel greatly	
conifler / esconifler }	to loiter about, dawdle	
corcobiar	to prance; work hard	(Sp. corcovear)
cosqueliser	to make a laughing-stock of	
drivaïer	to wander about, be a vagabond	(dériver)
fēl	to fail	(Eng.)
fouter	to strike, beat; cast down violently; give in a rude manner	
gâouler †	to romp	(garruleux)
gouroupier	to curry favour	(croupier)
graffiñèn, graffiller	to scratch	(griffoner)
janjcler	to twist, wriggle	
lainder	to beat, strike violently	
mâchicoter	to tear or crush in pieces	(mâchicatoire)
macнucar	to smash	(Sp. machucar)
marecager	to entangle, involve	(marécage)
maconnèn	to sew or tie clumsily	
mèk-mèk	to mince matters	(Eng. make make)
rodaïer	to ramble about	(roder)
saggaïer	to ransack; cut in pieces	(saccager)
santourar	to bless; *ironically*, to abuse	(Sp. santoral)

---

* The Creoles in speaking use the interjection cнens! obviously the French *tiens!* which is commonly employed in the same way; thus, cнéns! moèn cнémber zombi'i, hold! I have found him out, Fr. *tiens! je l'ai surpris dans ses ruses.*

† For gaoulèx. The artificial forms in this list are intended for the better discrimination of these words when they are verbs. We may here repeat that we usually adopt such forms whenever they appear to be necessary. For example, in the section containing Creole infinitives that are in reality French past participles, we have *couvèr, môr, ouvèr,* etc. for *couvert, mort, ouvert,* etc, these latter forms being reserved for use as participles.

Creole.	English.	French.
simier	to prefer	(*ce serait mieux ?*)
toriar	to bait bulls, etc.	(Sp. *torear*)
lounaïer	to turn frequently	(*tourner*)
*vaûmier**	same as *simier*	(*vaut mieux*)
vavoler	to whirl violently; hover; wallow	
vinaïer	to come often	(*venir*)
vonvonèn, vonvoner	to buzz	
wâte-wâte	to say " what, what"; i.e. to speak English	
-zéponèn	to spur	(*épéron*)

AUXILLIARIES.

Of all the Creole Auxilliaries, the most important and commonly used is *ca*. With regard to the origin of this word, we have not been able to discover anything satisfactory. But it is a verbal particle which denotes *progression* or *continuance*. Prefixed to a Verb, it forms the Present Tense Indicative, most usually with a progressive import; as, *yeaux* ca *déjinèn*, they *are breakfasting*, Fr. *ils* déjeunent. *Mi yon sépent* ca *tôtïer corps-li nans zebe la*, see there, a snake *is twisting* itself in the grass, Fr. *voilà un serpent qui se* tortille *dans l'herbe*. Denoting as it does the progress of an action, *ca* is also a sign of the Imperfect Indicative. But, in order to mark the past signification of this tense, *té*, an abbreviation of *étais*, or *était*, was, is prefixed to *ca*, forming the compound *té ca*, which is, in general, the characteristic of the Imperfect;—thus, *moèn* té ca *dodiner bord caïe la*, I *was loitering* near the house, Fr. *je* flanais *près de cette maison*.

SHALL or WILL, the future sign, is expressed in Creole, as often in French, by means of the verb *aller*, to go : but only under the forms *c'aller* (i.e. *ca aller*), *cäër*, and *va ('a)* ; e.g : *nous* c'aller *dïe li ça*, we *shall* tell him (or her) that, Fr. *nous lui* dirons *cela*.

SHOULD or WOULD (conditional) is represented by *sé*, an abbreviation of *serais*, or *serait*, conditional of *être*, to be. When

---

* See note on *gaouler*, preceding page.

auxilliary, *sé* loses its radical substantive meaning, and retains only the modal sense of *should* or *would;* as, *li pas* sé *fair* ça, he *would* not do (or have done) that, Fr. *il n'aurait pas fait cela.* But before Adjectives and Past Participles, *sé* resumes its legitimate import; e.g: *baggaie la pas* sé *bon, si zótes pas té ranger li,* the thing *would* not *be* (or *have been*) good, if you had not arranged it, Fr. *la chose ne* serait *pas bonne, si vous ne l'aviez pas arrangé. Lette la pas* sé *écrit,* the letter *would* not *be* (or *have been)* written, Fr. *la lettre ne* serait *pas écrite.*

SHOULD HAVE and WOULD HAVE may also be rendered by *sé,* as might be seen in the foregoing examples; but the most appropriate mode of expressing these auxilliaries is by means of the combination *sé va;* for instance, *li* sé va *aller, si nous té lésser li fair* cnér *li,* he *would have* gone, had we allowed him to follow his inclination, Fr. *il* aurait *allé, si nous lui avions permis de suivre son inclination.* Sometimes *té va* is used in the sense of *should* or *would have.* See conjugation of *manger.*

CAN in Creole is *sa,* which, like *save,* to know, is an abbreviation of the French *savent,* 3rd person plural Indicative of *savoir.* Like the English "can," *savoir* and its Creole corruption, *sa,* properly denote ability resulting from *knowledge;* e.g: *moèn* sa *danser,* I *can* (i.e. *know* how to) dance, Fr. *je* sais *danser.* But neither in Creole nor in English is this restriction observed.

MAY, denoting *permission* in English, is represented by *pé,* a corruption of *peux,* or *peut,* part of the French *pouvoir,* to be able. Although a distinction is seldom made in the dialect between *pé* and *sa,* we are yet of opinion that it would be preferable to use the former in cases where the sense of the verb is *permissive;* for example,—*moèn* sa *danser, main moèn* pé *pas fair li apouésent, páce moèn en déï,* I *can* dance, but I *may* not do it now, because I am in mourning. *Ous* sa *aller,* you *can* (i.e. *are able* to) go: *ous* pé *aller,* you *may* (i.e. are *permitted* to) go.

MAY HAVE or MIGHT HAVE is expressed by means of the combination *sé pé;* thus,—*Jean* sé pé *aller avant soléï té coucher;* Jean *may* (or *might*) *have* gone before the sun had set, Fr. *Jean* aurait pu *aller avant le coucher du soleil.*

COULD and MIGHT, as preterites of CAN and MAY, are respectively *té sa* and *té pé.* Like *sé,* when auxilliary, *té* loses its substantive meaning, and serves as a mere sign of past time; as, *nous* té sa *écrî; main nous oblier,* we *could* write, but have forgotten, Fr. *nous* pouvions *écrire, mais nous l'avons oublier.*

MUST is rendered in Creole, as in French, by means of the verb *falloir,* to be necessary. But the only forms employed in the dialect are *faut, fallait,* and, more rarely, *faudrait* and *faudra.* As impersonals, *fallait* and *faudrait* might have been allowed to retain their orthography, but it seems more correct to write them *fallé* and *faudré,* as pronounced by all ordinary speakers. For examples of their use, see conjugation of *manger.*

MUST HAVE is *té doé* or *doé té;* e.g: *li* té doé *ouèr ça;* or, better still, *li* doé té *ouér ça,* he *must have* seen that. The former construction may mean, "he *ought* to have seen that;" but the latter presents no ambiguity.

There is also another locution meaning *must have;* viz: *mañèn* or *mañèn té;* thus, *chén la* mañèn *voèr quéchoïe,* the dog *must have* seen something; *ous* mañèn té *die li ça,* you *must have* told him so. Sometime, though seldom, the French construction with *aura* is employed; as, *li* aura *té ouèr li ca batte bas,* he *must have* seen him in reduced circumstances.

LET, though not strictly speaking an auxilliary, may be allowed some notice here. This verb is represented in Creole by *léssez,* Fr. *laissez;* as, *léssez-moèn die ous, let* me tell you, Fr. *laissez-moi vous dire.* The Imperatives of *quitter* and *aller* (the latter under the form of *anouns,* for *allons*), are also used in the sense of *let,* but there is a distinction in the meaning conveyed by the use of each. *Anouns* is employed only in the *first person plural,* and is an invitation; thus, — anouns *chapper corps-nous, let* us escape, Fr. échappons-*nous.* *Quittes* and *léssez* are requests for permission to do the action expressed by the verb they govern; as, quittez *(or* léssez*) yeaux pousser blague yeaux, let* (or *allow*) them (to) have their chat, Fr. qu'*ils* aient *leur blague.* In conjugating *manger,* we give more than one person in the Imperative, but merely as a matter of practical convenience; for we are aware that *anouns*, *quittez*, and *léssez* are not there auxilliaries, but principal verbs governing *manger* in the Infinitive Mood.

MOODS.

The Mood of a Verb is the manner in which it is used.

When a Verb asserts, whether affirmatively or negatively, it is said to be in the INDICATIVE MOOD ; as *macaque* connaîte *qui bois li ea mouter*, monkey *knows* what sort of tree he *climbs*, Fr. *le singe sait sur quelle arbre il faut grimper. La fimèn pas ca sôtî sans difé,* smoke *does* not *issue* without fire, Fr. *pas de fumée sans feu.*

When a Verb expresses an action in a doubtful, qualified manner, it is said to be in the SUBJUNCTIVE MOOD ; as, *si lamer* té ca *chécher*, *if* the sea *were* to dry up; Fr. *si la mer* allait *sécher.*

A Verb is in the IMPERATIVE MOOD when it commands or requests ; as, bad'nèn *bien épis macaque, main* pouengâde *mañèn lacné li, joke* with a monkey as much as you please, but *beware* of handling his tail, Fr. amusez-*vous tant que voudriez avec le singe, mais* prenez-garde *de lui tirer la queue.*

A Verb expressing an action in a general, indeterminate, manner, without any reference to an agent, is said to be in the INFINITIVE MOOD ; as, *ricanèn*, to giggle, *créoliser*, to creolise.

TENSES.

Tense means time.

The Present Tense of a Verb denotes an action going on in present time ; as, *li* ca amblouser *pór bougue la*, he *is humbugging* the poor fellow, Fr. *il* trompe *ce pauvre diable.*

A Verb is said to be in the Imperfect Tense when it expresses an action as *going on* in past time ; as, *yeaux* té ca baîe *blow la lhér moèn river*, they *were relating* the incident when I arrived, Fr *ils* racontaient *cette affaire lorsque j'arrivai.*

When we speak of an action done in the past, without any reference to its progress or duration, the Verb denoting such action is said to be in the Preterite or l'ast Indefinite Tense ; as, *moèn* voèr *li ca casser bois nans zoreies li*, I *saw* he was obstinate, Fr. *je* vis *qu'il s'obstinait.*

An action which *is to* take place, is expressed by the Future-Tense; as, *ous* c'aller batte *li yon baboule*, you *will tell* him a cock-and-bull story, Fr. *vous lui* direz *des sornettes.*

The specialities of the Present and Past Perfect Tenses are, that they denote action *completed,* the former *at present,* and the latter *in time past;* e.g: Pres. Perf. *moèn* voèr *ça déjà,* I have *seen* that already, Fr. j'ai *déjà* vu *cela :*—Past. Perf. *nous* té *jà* ouèr *ça,* we *had* already *seen* that, Fr. *nous* avions *déjà* vu *cela.*

CONJUGATION.

The Verbs in Creole come under two classes or Conjugations. The first, and by far the largest, comprehends all verbs that form the Present and Imperfect Indicative with *ca*; the second, which may be called Irregular, comprises about twenty verbs that either do not admit, or commonly dispense with, that auxilliary in the formation of those tenses.

Conjugation with *ca :*—*Manger*, To Eat.

Indicative Mood—Present Tense.

SINGULAR.

Creole.	English.	French.
1. *moèn ca manger*	I eat, *or* am eating	*je mange*
2. *ous ca manger*	you eat, *or* are eating	*vous mangez*
3. *li,* (*'i) ca manger*	he, she eats, *or* is eating	*il, elle mange*

PLURAL.

1. *nous ca manger*	we eat, *or* are eating	*nous mangeons*
2. *zôtes ca manger*	you eat, *or* are eating	*vous mangez*
3. *yeaux ca manger*	they eat, *or* are eating	*ils, elles mangent*

Imperfect Tense.

SINGULAR.

1. *moèn té ca manger*	I was eating	*je mangeais*
2. *ous té ca manger*	you were eating	*vous mangiez*
3. *li, ('i) té ca manger*	he, she was eating	*il, elle mangeait*

PLURAL.

Creole.	English.	French.
1. *nous té ca manger*	we were eating	*nous mangions*
2. *zôtes té ca manger*	you were eating	*vous mangiez*
3. *yeaux té ca manger*	they were eating	*ils, elles mangeaient*

Preterite and Perfect Tenses.

SINGULAR.

Creole.	English.	French.
1. *moèn manger*	I ate, *or* have eaten	*je mangeai,* or *ai mangé*
2. *ous manger*	you ate, *or* have eaten	*vous mangeâtes,* or *avez mangé*
3. *li, ('i) manger*	he, she ate, *or* have eaten	*il, elle mangea,* or *a mangé*

PLURAL.

Creole.	English.	French.
1. *nous manger*	we ate, *or* have eaten	*nous mangeâmes,* or *avons mangé*
2. *zôtes manger*	you ate, *or* have eaten	*vous mangeâtes,* or *avez mangé*
3. *yeaux manger*	they ate, *or* have eaten	*ils, elles mangèrent,* or *ont mangé*

Past Perfect Tense.

SINGULAR.

Creole.	English.	French.
1. *moèn té manger*	I had eaten	*j'avais,* or *eus mange*
2. *ous té manger*	you had eaten	*vous aviez,* or *eûtes mangé*
3. *li té manger*	he or she had eaten	*il, elle avait,* or *eut mangé*

PLURAL.

Creole.	English.	French.
1. *nous té manger*	we had eaten	*nous avions,* or *eûmes mangé*
2. *zôtes té manger*	you had eaten	*vous aviez,* or *eûtes mangé*
3. *yeaux té manger*	they had eaten	*ils, elles avaient,* or *eurent mangé*

Future Tense.

SINGULAR.

Creole.	English.	French.
1. *moèn c'aller manger*	I will (*or* am going to) eat	*je mangerai*
2. *ous c'aller manger*	you shall (*or* are going to) eat	*vous mangerez*
3. *li, ('i) c'aller manger*	he, she will (*or* is going to) eat	*il, elle mangera*

PLURAL.

Creole.	English.	French.
1. *nous c'aller manger*	we shall, etc. eat	*nous mangerons*
2. *zôtes c'aller manger*	ye will, etc. eat	*vous mangerez*
3. *yeaux c'aller manger*	they shall, etc. eat	*ils mangeront*

Other Forms.

SINGULAR.

1. *moèn cãër manger*	I am going to eat	*je vais manger*
2. *ous va manger*	you are going to eat	*vous allez manger*
3. *'i cãër,* or *li 'a manger*	he, she shall eat	*il, elle va manger*

PLURAL.

1. *nous va manger*	we are going to eat	*nous allons manger*
2. *zôtes cãër manger*	you will eat	*vous allez manger*
3. *yeaux va manger*	they are going to eat	*ils, elles vont manger*

Conditional Mood—Present Tense.

SINGULAR.

1. *moèn sé manger*	I should eat	*je mangerais*
2. *ous sé manger*	you would eat	*vous mangeriez*
3. *li ('i) sé manger*	he, she would eat	*il, elle mangerait*

PLURAL.

1. *nous sé manger*	we should eat	*nous mangerions*
2. *zôtes sé manger*	you would eat	*vous mangeriez*
3. *yeaux sé manger*	they should eat	*ils mangeraient*

Past Tense.

SINGULAR.

1. *moèn sé va manger*	I should have eaten	*j'aurais mangé*
2. *ous sé 'a manger*	you would have eaten	*vous auriez mangé*
3. *li ('i) sé va manger*	he, she would have eaten	*il, elle aurait mangé*

PLURAL.

1. *nous sé 'a manger*	we should have eaten	*nous aurions mangé*
2. *zôtes sé va manger*	you should have eaten	*vous auriez mangé*
3. *yeaux sé va manger*	they should have eaten	*ils auraient mangé*

Another Form.

Creole.	English.	French.

SINGULAR.

1. *moèn té va manger*	should have eaten	*j'aurais mangé*
2. *ous té 'a manger*	you would have eaten	*vous auriez mangé*
3. *li, (i) té 'a manger*	he, she would have eaten	*il, elle aurait mangé*

PLURAL.

1. *nous té 'a manger*	we would have eaten	*nous aurions mangé*
2. *zôtes té va manger*	you should have eaten	*vous auriez mangé*
3. *yeaux té 'a manger*	they would have eaten	*ils auraient mangé*

Imperative Mood.

SINGULAR.

2. *mangez !* *	eat !	*mangez !*
3. *léssez-li manger !*	let him eat !	*qu'il mange !*

PLURAL.

1. *anouns manger*	let us eat	*mangeons*
2. *mangez ! zôtes mangez !*	eat ! eat ye !	*mangez !*
3. *quittez-yeaux manger*	let them eat	*qu'ils mangent !*

Subjunctive Mood—Present Tense.

SINGULAR.

1. *si moèn manger*	if I eat	*si je mangeais, etc.*
2. *si ous manger*	if you eat	
3. *si li manger*	if he, *or* she eat	

---

* Such departures from the infinitive form as those in the text, are purely artificial: the Creole being essentially non-inflecting. The notion that there may be an imperative form in the dialect is suggested by the identity of the sound of *ez* (the termination of that Mood) with the Creole pronunciation of *er*. But if we turn to those verbs whose final sounds are dissimilar to that of *er*, we find in every case that the same sound heard in the Infinitive prevails throughout all the other Moods. As instances take *fimèn, tounèn, coude, joène, pende, vive,* etc.

Creole.	English.	French.

PLURAL.

1. *mâgré nous manger*	altho' we eat	*quoique nous mangions, etc.*
2. *mâgré zôtes manger*	altho' you eat	
3. *mâgré yeaux manger*	altho' they eat	

Past Tense.

1. *quand-même moèn té manger*	even tho' I ate	*même si je mangeais, etc.*
2. *quand-même ous té manger*	even tho' you ate	
3. *quand-même 'i té manger*	even tho' he, she ate	

PLURAL.

1. *quoèqui nous té manger*	altho' we ate, (had eaten)	*quoique nous ayons mangé, etc.*
2. *quoèqui zôtes té manger*	altho' you ate	
3. *quoèqui yeaux té manger*	altho' they had eaten	

Potential Mood—Present Tense.

SINGULAR.

1. *moèn sa (*or *pé) manger*	I can *or* may eat	*je puis manger*
2. *ous sa (*or *pé) manger*	you can *or* may eat	*vous pouvez manger*
3. *si sa (*or *pé) manger*	he, she can *or* may eat	*il, elle peut manger*

PLURAL.

1. *nous sa (*or *pé) manger*	we can *or* may eat	*nous pouvons manger*
2. *zotes sa (*or *pé) manger*	you can *or* may eat	*vous pouvez manger*
3. *yeaux sa (*or *pé) manger*	they can *or* may eat	*ils, elles peuvent manger*

Another Form.

SINGULAR.

1. *faut moèn manger*	I must eat	*il faut que je mange*
2. *faut ous manyer*	you must eat	*il faut que vous mangiez*
3. *faut li manger*	he, she must eat	*il faut qu'il mange*

PLURAL.

1. *faut nous manger*	we must eat	*il faut que nous mangions*
2. *faut zôtes manger*	you must eat	*il faut que vous mangiez*
3. *faut yeaux manger*	they must eat	*il faut qu'ils mangent*

| Creole. | English. | French. |

Past Tense.

SINGULAR.

1. *moèn té sa manger*	I could eat	*je pouvais manger*
2. *ous té pé manger*	you might eat	*vous pouviez manger*
3. *si té sa manger*	he, she could eat	*il, elle pouvait manger*

PLURAL.

1. *nous té pé manger*	we could eat	*nous pourions manger*
2. *zôtes té sa manger*	you could eat	*vous pouviez manger*
3. *yeaux té pé manger*	they could eat	*ils, elles ont pu manger*

Perfect and Pluperfect Tenses.

SINGULAR.

1. *moĕn sé pé manget*	I may or might have eaten	*j'aurai pu manger, etc.*
2. *ous sé pé manger*	you may or might have eaten	
3. *li sé pé manger*	he (or she) may or might have eaten	

PLURAL.

1. *nous sé pé mangev*	we might have eaten	*nous aurions pu manger, etc.*
2. *zôtes sé pé manger*	you may have eaten	
3. *yeaux sé pé manger*	they might have eaten	

Infinitive Mood—Present Tense.

Manger—To Eat.

Past Tense.

Poú té manger—To have eaten—*Avoir mangé.*

Participles.

PRES.—*Mangeant*—Eating.

PAST —*Mangé*—Eaten.

Conjugation of a Verb without *ca.*

Aimèn—To Love—*Aimer.*

Indicative Mood—Present Tense.

SINGULAR.

Creole.	English.	French.
1. *moèn aimèn*	I love	*j'aime*
2. *ous aimèn*	you love	*vous aimez.*
3. *li aimèn*	he, she loves	*il, elle aime*

PLURAL.

Creole.	English.	French.
1. *nous aimèn*	we love	*nous aīmons*
2. *zôtes aimèn*	you love	*vous aimez*
3. *yeaux aimèn*	they love	*ils, elles aiment*

Imperfect, Preterite, and Past Perfect Tenses.

SINGULAR.

Creole.	English.	French.
1. *moèn té aimèn*	I loved, had loved	*j'aimais, avais, eus aimé*
2. *ous té aimèn*	you loved, had loved	*vous aimiez, aviez, eûtes aimé*
3. *i té aimèn*	he, she loved, had loved	*il, elle aimait, avait, eut aimé*

PLURAL.

Creole.	English.	French.
1. *nous té aimèn*	we loved, had loved	*nous avions aimé, etc.*
2. *zôtes té aimèn*	you loved, did love	*vous aimâtes, etc.*
3. *yeaux té aimèn*	they loved, had loved	*ils, elles eurent aimé, etc.*

These are, as before remarked, the only tenses in which the two
Conjugations differ. Besides *aimèn*, the other verbs thus conjugated
are :—

Creole.	English.	French.
bisoèn	to need	*avoir besoin (de)*
compter	to intend	
connaite	to know	*connaître, savoir*
content	to like	*aimer, être content (de)*

Creole.	English.	French.
doé *	ought	*devoir*
envie	to long	*avoir envie (de)*
foubièn *pas foubièn* }	not to care	
häï	to hate	*häir*
honte	to be ashamed	*avoir honte, être honteux, (de)*
jaloû	to envy, to be jealous of	*être jaloux (de)*
mériter	to deserve	
pé	to be able	*pouvoir*
pouéférer	to prefer	*préférer*
sa	to be able	*pouvoir (savoir)*
save	to know	*savoir*
simiér	to prefer	*preferer*
soucier	not to care (seldom to care)	
tinî	to have, hold	*avoir, tenir*
vail	to be worth	*valoir*
vaûmier	to prefer, have rather	
vlé†	to wish, want	*vouloir*

INTERROGATIVE AND NEGATIVE CONJUGATIONS.

To conjugate a Verb interrogatively, no peculiar construction is required : the tone of the voice being the usual mode of indicating the nature of a proposition :—thus, *moèn manger?* have I eaten? Fr. *ai-je mangé?* To employ the Verb negatively, *pas* must be put immediately after the Nominative; e. g.—*graisse pas tinî sentiment*, fatness is *not* fastidious, Fr. *la graisse n'a pas de sentiment*. To ask a question negatively, the foregoing construction, usually preceded by *éce*, is employed; as, *éce yeaux toutes pas coèr*, or simply, *yeaux toutes pas coèr?* did they not all believe? Fr. *n'ont-ils pas tous cru?* The following are examples of these two modes of construction :—

Vlé, Tinî, Save, Doé.

* *Doé*, meaning to *owe*, is also conjugated with *ca*; e. g. *li ca doé moèn yon lâgent*, he owes me some money, Fr. *il me doît de l'argent*.

† In the Syntax of Verbs the reader will see in what cases these words are constructed with *ca*.

Indicative Mood—Present Tense.

Creole.	French.	English.

SINGULAR.

1- *êce moèn vlé ?*	do I want ?	*cst-ce que je veux ?* etc.
2. *êce ous vlé ?*	do you wish ?	
3. *êce li vlé ?*	does he want ?	

PLURAL.

1. *êce nous tnî ?*	have we ?	*avons-nous ?* etc.
2. *êce zôtes tnî ?*	have you ?	
3. *êce yeaux tnî ?*	have they ?	

and so on through all the Moods and Tenses.

Save — To Know — *Doé* — To Owe.

Indicative Mood—Present Tense.

Creole.	English.	French.

SINGULAR.

1. *moèn pas save*	I do not know	*je ne sais pas, ete.*
2. *vous pas save*	you do not know	
3. *'i pas save*	he does not know	

PLURAL.

1. *nous pas ca doé*	we do not owe	*nous ne devons pas etc.*
2. *zôtes pas ca doé*	you do not owe	
3. *yeaux pas ca doé*	they do not owe	

REFLEXIVE CONJUGATION

Is performed by placing the Reflexive Pronouns immediately after the Verb, thus :—

Creole.	English.	French.
1. *moèn ca soèn corps-moèn*	I am caring myself	*je me soigne*
2. *ous content corps-ous*	you like yourself	*vous vous aimez*
3. *'i amboèse corps-li*	he concealed himself	*il s'est caché*

THE PASSIVE VOICE.

Owing to the absence of inflections, but, perhaps, chiefly to the want of a regular Substantive Verb, the Creole is essentially *subjective*. In fact, it may be broadly stated that a purely passive construction is never used in the dialect, except by persons in some measure acquainted with French. The Past Participles, which, in most languages, are the bases of passive constructions, have in general lost their verbal force and become pure adjectives; *être*, the verb *to be*, whereof only a few corruptions exist under the forms *té, sé, etc.*,* possesses its radical force only now and then. The passive phrases that can be formed by us are with *té* and *sé* alone; but, owing to the ambiguity that may arise from employing them in this way, we usually construct our sentences *actively*. For example: *he is loved*, Cr. yeaux *aimèn li, they love him*. If we say *li aimèn* simply, the expression would unavoidably be understood as, *he loves;* similarly, *nous sé soupouende*, would mean, *we would surprise;* but a passive locution may be formed by adding a complement to the sentence: thus, *nóus sé soupouende pâ ces mounes la*, we would *be* surprised by those people, Fr. *nous serions surpris par ces gens-là.* Constructions of this kind are evidently French, and should seldom be used, as they are not only grotesque, but ambiguous as well.

TRANSITIVES AND INTRANSITIVES.

Most verbs in Creole may be used transitively; that is to say, with an accusative after them. This arises chiefly from the general suppression of the monosyllables used in French to denote the reflexive or intransitive nature of certain verbs. Each of the following, for instance, though governing an accusative in Creole, requires both the reflexive pronoun and a preposition for their correct employment in French :—

---

* For further remarks on the verb *to be*, Idiomatic constructions of the Verbs, etc., see Syntax of the Verbs and List of Idioms.

Creole.	English.	French.
entende misique	to understand music	*s'entendre en musique*
chapper yon volée	to escape a thrashing	*s'échapper d'une castigation*
mãïer yon fîe	to marry a girl	*se marier à une fille*
moCHer grands mounes	to ridicule elderly folk	*se moquer des grandes per-sonnes*

From the above examples it will be seen that the omission in Creole of *se*, *à* and *de*, alters the relation between verbs and their dependant cases, and makes direct regimens of these last.

There are, however, some verbs which, from the meaning they convey, or by the decision of custom, cannot be used transitively in Creole, viz. ;—

assise, to sit; *domî*, to sleep; *gdouler*, to romp; *môr*, to die; *pâtî*, to start; *pé*, to be able; *rodaïer*, to dawdle about; *sa*, can; *sôtî*, to go out; *ravoter*, to revolve; *vinî*, to come; *vive*, to live; etc.

IMPERSONALS.

The Creoles employ *fair*, to make, in combination with certain adjectives, to describe impersonally the state of the weather or atmosphere. The invariable nominative of the impersonals thus formed is *'i*, it, which is more generally dropped than expressed in conversation. We subjoin the impersonals :—

Creole.	English.	French.
(i) ca fair beautemps	it is fairweather	*il fait beau*
té ca fair bouin	it was dusk	*c'était sur la brune*
(i) té fair chaud	it was warm	*il faisait chaud*

To which we must add *fair clair*, to be light; *fair foète*, to be cold; *fair noèr*, to be dark; and also *fair soleî*, to be sunny.

ADVERBS.

An Adverb is joined to a Verb, an Adjective, or another Adverb, to qualify or to express some circumstance respecting it; as, *'i ca doloter*

iches li toûplein,* he coddles his children *a great deal*, Fr, *Il dorlote
beaucoup ses enfants ;—madame la tini yon lair* touô' *dendé poú moèn*, that
lady has *too* determined an air for me, Fr. *cette dame à l'air* trop
déterminé pour moi ;—yon fois cé poú coud-coud, li 'a vini bien vitement,
so its for a feed, he will come *very quickly*, Fr. *pourvu que ce soit pour
manger, il viendra* bien vite. The Adverbs are mostly the same as in
French. Those that are peculiar will appear in the ensuing list.

As in French and English, adjectives are often used adverbially ; e.g. :—

> Cr. *Conça, 'i pâler* gras *ba yeaux, ein ?*
> Eng. So, he spoke *fat* (i.e. *boastfully*) to them, did he ?
> Cr. *Tit mammaïe la ca fair toute-baggaie* douôle.
> Eng. The (that) child does everything *droll* (i.e. *strangely.)*
> Fr. *Cet enfant fait toutes choses drôlement.*

LIST OF ADVERBS.

Of Time.

Creole.	English.	French.
à-la-fois	at once, at a time	*à la fois*
apoués	after	*après*
apoués dèmain	day after to-morrow	*après demain*
apoués-mindi	in the afternoon	*après midi*
àpouésent	now, at present	*à présent*
aussitot, sitot	as soon as, soon	*aussitôt*
avant	before, beforehand	*(auparavant)*
avant-hier, avant-zier	day before yesterday	*avant hier*
belle-drive	a long while ago	
bientot	soon	*bientôt*
cnêquefois	sometimes	*quelquefois*
déjà, 'ja	already	*déjà*
dèmain	to-morrow	*demain*
dré-en-avant	from henceforth	*dorenavant*
dri	often	*(dru)*
encor	again	

* For *tout plein.*

Creole.	English.	French.
encor (after pas)	any more	
ensouite	afterwards	*ensuite*
jadis, or rather *nans temps jadis*	formerly	*jadis*
jamain	never	*jamais*
lhêr	when	*(à l'heure que)*
lôte-fois, lézôtes-fois	formerly, in ancient times	*autrefois*
pâncor, pôncer	not yet	*pas encore*
pîtot	sooner, rather	*plutôt*
quant-et-quant (t sounded)	at the same time, simultaneously	
râment	rarely, seldom	*rarement*
soudainement	suddenly	
souvent, souventment	often	*souvent*
tandis, tandîque	whilst	*tandis que*
tantot	by and by	*tantôt*
tantot-là	a little while since	
temps	when	
to'-o-tâd	sooner or later	*tot ou tard*
tous-lé-mouments	every minute	*tous les moments*
toujoûs	always, still	*toujours*
tous-lé-joûs	every day	*tous les jours*
tout-à-lhêr	just now, presently	*tout-à-l'heure*
toû-souite	directly	*tout de suite*

Of Place.

Creole.	English.	French.
à-coté	aside, away	
à-doète	to the right	*à droite*
au-fond	to the bottom	
à-gôche	to the left	
alliêrs	elsewhere	*ailleurs*
alentoû, lentoû	round about	*alentour*
à-pât	apart, separately	*à part*
au-poués	near by	*au près*
coté? qui coté?	where.? whither?	*quel coté?*
déhors, déouors	outside	*dehors*
déièr	behind	*derrière*

Creole.	English.	French.
dicite, dicite-ici	from here	*d'ici*
en-avant	forwards	
en-bas	below	
en-èrièr	backwards	*en arrière*
en-haut	aloft, above	
en-lair	above, atop	*(en l'air)*
Jisse *Jouque* *Jousse* } *icite*	up to here	*jusqu'ici*
jousse ôti ?	how far ?	*jusqu'où ?*
là	there	
là-bas-là	yonder	*là-bas*
lоèn	afar	*loin*
ôti	where	*où (es-tu ?)*
poués	near	*près*
pouôche	near by	*proche*

Of Manner.

Creole.	English.	French.
à-corps-dort-à-corps-vêî	cautiously	*à corps dort à corps veille*
à-coubà	clumsily ; schemingly	
à-dàdà	astride	
à-lassaut	unawares	*(à l'assaut)*
à-lenvers	wrong-side-out	*à l'envers*
au-biɢoule	to perfection	
bien	well	
cabà-cabà	clumsily	
сon, comme	like, as	*comme*
ıon ça même	in like manner	*(comme cela même)*
сoument	how	
coument coument	at all events, however	*comment*
соuñan-couñan *cuñan-cañan* }	slowly	
d: suite	successively	*de suite*
d-vient ? doù-vient ?	how comes it (that) ?	*d'où vient ?*
ех-balan	swayingly	
ев-bène en-bène	furtively, sneakingly	*(Eng. bend)*
ев-biés	slanting, athwart	

Creole.	English.	French.
en-biscade	covertly	*(ambuscade)*
en-bouloque	higgledy piggledy	
ensembe	together	*ensemble*
espoués	purposely	*exprès*
mal, malment, malouque	badly	*mal*
miéx	better	*mieux*
pâfôce	forcibly, reluctantly	*par force*
pêle-mêle, en pêque-mêle	confusedly	*pêle mêle*
piame-piame	so so, by degrees	
poc-a-poc (Sp.)	gradually, little by little	
ric-à-rac	up to the brim	*ric à ric*
sang foéte	calmly, in cool blood	*de sang froid*
sans fôte	without fail	*sans faute*
sans honte	shamelessly	
sans pidèr	immodestly	*sans pudeur*
sîtout	especially	*surtout*
so-so (Eng.)	indifferently	
tant-soet-pé	very little, however small	*(tant soit peu)*
tout-din-coup	all of a sudden	*(tout d'un coup)*
touop	too, too much	*trop*
touop pé	too little	*trop peu*
tout-à-faite	altogether, entirely	*tout à fait*
yon-fois	at once	*(une fois)*

Of Affirmation, Denial, &c.

Creole.	English.	French.
absoliment, assoliment	assuredly	*absolument*
à-coup-sî	of course	*à coup sûr*
aussi	also	
bien sî	very true	*bien sûr*
çasse-pé	perhaps	*cela se peut*
cêtèlement	certainly	*certainement*
coument nonc ?	how so ? most decidedly	*comment donc ?*
jamain	never	*jamais*
na (in songs)	(do) not	*ne*
non	no	
non coument	no indeed	

Creole.	English.	French.
Pas	not	
Pas pièce	not at all	
Pêtête	perhaps	*peut être*
Poû-toute-bon, toute-bon	really, in good sooth	*(pour tout de bon)*
sans doute	doubtless	
sans die mentî	truly	*(sans dire mentir)*

Of Quantity, Number, &c.

Creole	English	French
à-bime-so	abundantly	
assez	enough	
assez con ça	a pretty good deal	
au-moens	at least	*au moins*
autant	as many, as much	
beaucoup	a great deal, a great many	
commèn, combé	how many	*combien*
di-plis	in excess	*de plus*
encor	more	
en-pile	much, a great deal	*en pile*
*Gèr (*with *pas)*	(not) much	*guère*
gran-choïe	much	*grand'chose*
ho-to-to	in abundance	
moènce	less	*moins*
pé	few, little	*peu*
plis	more	*plus*
tant	so much	

PREPOSITIONS.

Prepositions are put before the words they govern, to show the relation which these words bear to others, as :—

Cr.   *Béf* nans *côde cé* * *poû* CHOUER.

·Eng.   Ox *in* rope is to (be) killed.

Fr.   *Bœuf* à *la corde est pour être tué.*

* This word represents the French *c'est*, it is ; but as neither *ce* nor *est* is used singly in Creole, and as the combination *c'est* does duty for the verb *to be*, we shall in future adhere to the spelling given above, for reasons already stated at pages 12 and 47.

Cr.   *Lire muèn* endidans *sac ous.*
Eng.   My book (is) *in* your bag.
Fr.   *Mon livre est* dans *votre sac.*

The following list contains the prepositions commonly used in Creo

Creole.	English.	French.
à-ce-poil	as to, with regard to	
alentoû, lentoû	around, about	*(alentour)*
apouès	after	*après*
avant	before	
compte	about, with regard to	*sur compte de*
conte	against	*contre*
déïèr	behind	*derrière*
dépîs	since	*depuis*
di	of	*de*
dici, dicite	from	*d'ici*
dirant, dirant temps	whilst	*durant*
en	in	
en-bas	under, beneath	
en-didans	within	*(en dedans)*
en-Gise	instead of	*(en guise de)*
en-haut	above	
en-tirant	excepting	
en-travers	across	
ente	between	*entre*
envers	towards	
épîs *	with	
excepté, cepté	except	*excepté*
fôte	for want of	*faute de*
hôde	out of	*hors de*
jique, jisse, jouque, jousse	up to	*jusque*
lacaïe	at the house of	
la-sous	upon, on	*(la-dessus)*
lôte-bôd	beyond	*(à l'autre bord de)*

* *épis*, with, so spelt to distinguish it from *et-pis*, and—both representi
the French connective *et puis*, and then, after that, etc.

Creole.	English.	French.
mâgré	in spite of	malgré
nans	in	dans
'nans mitan	amidst	
pâ	by	par
pâmi	amongst	parmi
pendant, pennant	while	pendant
poû	for	pour
poués	near	près
sans	without	
sôve	save	sauf
silon, soulon	according to	selon
suivant	according to	
vis-à-vis	opposite	

CONJUNCTIONS.

Conjunctions join words and sentences together; as, *moèn et-pìs fouèr nous*, I *and* our brother, Fr. *moi* et *notre frère;* '*i sé crier ça yon gênement*, si '*i té nans chimèn li*, he would have called that an obstacle, *if* it were in his path, Fr. *il aurait appeler cela un obstacle, s'il se trouvait dans son chemin.*

The Conjunctions usually heard in Creole are :—

Creole.	English.	French.
ainsi, alosse	so, therefore	(ainsi, alors)
avant	rather than	(avant de)
conça	so, therefore	(comme cela)
davoèr	because	(d'avoir)
et, et-pîs	and	(et puis)
mâgré	although	malgré
mâgré-si	however if	
ni—ni	neither—nor	
o, obèn	or	(ou, ou bien)
pâce	because	parceque
si	if	

Creole.	*English.*	*French.*
soct—o, svet—obèn	either—or	*soit*
pîsse	since	*puisque*
poûtant	yet	*pourtant*
nonc	then, therefore	*donc*

INTERJECTIONS.

Interjections are ejaculations by which we give vent to sudden emotions; as,

Oui foute! *li flambé!*   Oh dear! he is done for!

In Creole there is an infinitude of these ejaculations.   To attempt to translate them, as is done in some books, is simply absurd; inasmuch as the correct rendering of any of them by a particular expression must depend upon tones and other circumstances which no grammar can take into account.   We content ourselves, therefore, with submitting a few examples, under head of the emotion which *most usually* gives utterance them :—

Anger :—*cri blé! tombeau! toulouse! tempon! tonnèr, tonnèr di sort! tonnèr di boèse! tonnèr mécou! tonnèr mélengue! tôtie, tôtie tèr! sanicoton! etc.*

Joy :—*bouavo! hourré! bien! etc.*

Grief :—*aie! aie aie aie! hélas! woï! etc.*

Apprehension :—*ouî foute! ouî pipe! oui maman! etc.*

Surprise :—*ah ah! eh eh! oh oh! eh bèn! etc.*

DIALECTIC DEVELOPMENTS.

Spoken as it is by thousands upon thousands of human beings, to most of whom all other language is unknown, the Creole would have been a singular dialect indeed, if, from its formation up to the present time, it had continued to be a mere jumble of French words, uncouthly pronounced, and, at best, pervertedly understood. A language spoken and yet inert is an impossibility. Hence this rude patois, though abandoned to theignorant, and used only occasionally among instructed persons, yet exhibits one of.the vital characteristics of living tongues in its capability of generating new terms from radicals within itself. Of course, the operation of this procreating energy is but fitful and limited ; but to a true philologer it suggests a curious speculation on what the Creole might have been, were circumstances favourable to its independent growth and cultivation.

In the foregoing portions of this work we have given specimens of peculiar word-formations; but only in illustration of general statements, and without reference to the principles followed in the construction of those which are not mere corruptions but real developments of other forms. We will here offer a few remarks on these, but our attention will be confined to nouns and verbs, as they are more extensively formed in Creole than any other kinds of words.

NOUNS.

In framing nouns, generally from verbal roots, the most common termination is *ade ;* as, from

VERB.			NOUN.
dévirer	(Fr. *dévier*)	to turn back,	*dévirade*, a turning back.
boulevesser	(Fr. *bouleverser*)	to upturn,	*boulevessade*, an upturning.
rimèn	(Fr. *remuer*)	to stir,	*rimade*, a stirring.
soucrer	(Fr. *secouer*)	to shake,	*soucrade*, a shaking.

In fact, a great number of verbs may, by means of this termination, be converted into perfectly intelligible Creole nouns. Nor are these new formations superfluous, even when the legitimate derivatives are also used ; for these synonomous terms, in the lips of even the most ignorant, express those distinctions in a general idea which are so apt to be confounded. For example, the French substantive from *secouer*, to shake, is *secousse*, in Creole *soucousse*. The usual meaning of this word in Creole as in French, is, a shock, or sudden

agitation. The Creole *soucrade*, on the other hand, signifies a shaking.
Of course, the general notion of agitation adheres to both words; but
even they who cannot see the difference between a shaking and a shock,
could not fail to learn it,—from a little practical experience of both.
At all events, a Creole, if he has felt a shock, would say, *moèn sentì
yon* soucousse; but if he got a shaking, say, from the jolting of a cart,
moèn trapper yon soucrade, must be his language, or he will not
have said what he intended.

A little less common than *ade*, and often substituted for it, is the
noun-ending *age*, Creolicè *aïe*. But, unlike *ade*, which usually denotes the *act of doing*, *aïe* mostly signifies *the thing done*. The former answers, therefore, to the English *ing*, and the latter to *ion;* the
one often used for the other, as *age* or *aïe* is, in Creole, for *ade*. We
subjoin specimens of words in *aïe :—*

VERB.		NOUN.	
direr (Fr. durer*)* to last,		*la diraïe,*	duration.
velopper	to wind,	*veloppaïe,*	a winding or fold.
maron	to flee,	*maroùaïe*	flight
soucrer	to shake,	*soucraïe,*	agitation.
maconèn	to sew clumsily,	*maconaïe,*	a clumsy suture.

The other nominal terminations are *ment* and *té*, of which, we believe, the latter is most rarely used. In fact, the only words that we
have discovered with this ending, are *bouaveté*, bravery, from *bouave*,
brave (Fr. noun, *bravoure*): and *malté* distress from *mal*, in the Creole
sense of being "hard up," or in low circumstances. We find *ment* in
toûnement, a turning from *toûnèn*, Fr. *tourner*, to turn, *génement* obstacle, *impediment*, from *génèn*, (Fr. *géner*) to impede,—or, what is
not unlikely, *génement* might be formed from *géne* by apagoge of *ment*.

VERBS.

Exclusive of a number of verbs of genuine Creole growth, there are
a few from French etymons to which we shall devote a moment's attention. To be brief, we shall speak only of those constructed from
verbs; as they are somewhat curious. The termination of these, as

indeed of most verbs in the dialect, is *er*, which replaces whatever other ending the original verb may have. Between the termination and the root, the syllable *aï* is inserted, and this gives a frequentative meaning to the new formation ; e.g. :—

SIMPLE FORM.		FREQUENTATIVE.	
driver,	to stagger	*drivaïer*,	to stagger much.
rimèn,	to stir	*rimaïer*,	to agitate
toûnèn,	to turn	*tounaïer*,	to turn often
vinî,	to come	*vinaïer*,	to come frequently.

We here close the Second Part of this Grammar.   For a full and satisfactory discussion of individual words, the pages of a dictionary are the most fitting place.

PART III.

SYNTAX.

Syntax treats of the proper arrangement of words in sentences.

SENTENCES.

Before proceeding to the syntactical details of the Parts of Speech, we shall offer a few general remarks on the framing of sentences in Creole.

A sentence or proposition may be affirmative, negative, or interrogative.

AFFIRMATIVE SENTENCES.

When the subject of a proposition is followed by a simple attributive, by an adverb of place,—in short, by any word denoting its *quality*, *situation*, or *posture*, no substantive verb is employed in Creole as a connective, if present time is intended ; as,

Creole.	*English.*	*French.*
moèn bon,	I *am* good,	*je* suis *bon.*
ous malice,	you *are* cunning,	*vous* êtes *rusé.*
yeaux là,	they *are* there,	*ils* sont *là.*
li assise,	he *is* seated,	*il* est *assis.*

But if a noun, or any word representing it, follows in appositive relation to the subject, then *cé* comes in as copula, in the present tense ; as,

English.	*Creole.*	*French.*
nous cé *mounes*	we *are* human beings	*nous* sommes *humains*
zôtes cé *anglés,*	you *are* English people	*vous* êtes *anglais*

When the verb is in a compounded tense, the adverb does not, as generally in French, come between the auxilliary and principal verbs, but after the latter; as,

Cr. *Gens nous té ouèr* en-pile fois, our people had *often* seen, Fr. *nos gens avaient* souvent *vu; nous sé va connaîte zôtes* bien, we would have known *you well;* Fr. *nous vous aurions* bien *connus.*

When the verb has two regimens, a direct and an indirect, the latter must in Creole come first; as,

Cr. *Se-sé 'i ba* mounonque *nous baggaïe la,* his sister gave our *uncle* the *thing,* Fr. *sa sœur a donné l'objet à notre* oncle.

The French dative construction agrees with the Creole only in particular cases; as when the indirect regimen is a personal pronoun, etc.

NEGATIVE SENTENCES

Are formed by means of *pas,* which is supplemented by *jamain,* or by *pièce* according to circumstances, if there is no verb expressed. The place of *pas* is always after the subject or its accessories; but when there is a verb, it comes immediately before this last, whether simple or compounded; as,

Cr. *Moèn* pas *malice,* I am *not* cunning, Fr. *je* ne *suis* pas *rusé.*
Cr. *Joupa la qui nans place la* pas *grand,* the hut that is in the place (is) not large, Fr. *la cabane qui est dans ce lieu* n'*(est)* pas *grande.*
Cr. *Macaque* pas *ca die iche li laide,* monkey does *not* say its young is ugly, Fr. *le singe* ne *dit* pas *que ses petits sont laids.*

To strengthen a negative, *jamain* is often used with *pas;* as,

Cr. *Gens bon-temps* pas jamain *connaîte lhèr temps yeaux bon,* people (seeing) good times *never* know when their times are good, Fr. *les heureux* ne *savent* jamais *lorsqu'ils le sont.*

In compounded tenses, *jamain* generally comes between the auxilliary and principal verbs ; but it may sometimes precede the former ; as,

Cr. *Bombance pas ca* jamain *gañèn mêci*, or *pas jamain ca gañèn mêci*, extravagance never buys thanks, Fr. *la prodigalité* n'*achète* jamais *de remerciments.*

Pièce, coming in a sentence after *pas*, forms an absolute and total denial ; as,

Cr. *Ous pas piéter li* pièce, you did *not* follow him up *at all*, Fr. *vous ne l'avez* pas *épié* du tout.

This word, when thus used adverbially, must always follow the principal verb, the accusative or its accessories.

INTERROGATIVE SENTENCES.

We have, at page 61, explained that a question is asked in Creole either by the tone of the voice or by means of *éce* placed before the subject. With respect to sentences that have a present substantive import, no change of construction is required ; except when the question is asked by means of *qui moune, qui ça, ça*, etc., in which case *yé* * *(am, is, are)* must come after the subject or its accessories ; as, *qui moune ous* yé ? who *are* you, *qui* êtes *vous ?*

Cr. *Qui ça baggaïe la qui la-sous tabe la* yé ? what *is* that thing which is on the table ? Fr. *quel* est *l'objet qui est sur la* table ?

SYNTAX OF THE ARTICLES.

THE INDEFINITE ARTICLE.

The Indefinite Article, *yon*, is used in Creole, to denote a single indeterminate object ; as, yon *nômme ca môr*, *a* man dies, (Fr. un *homme meurt.*)

------

* From *yest* the Creole pronunciation of *est* is. See note on *yeaux*, page 12, and that on *cé*, page 69.

It is used in Creole, but not in French, before words, denoting, the nationality, rank, or calling of persons; as,

Cr. *Papa moèn pas* yon *fouancés*, my father is not *a* Frenchman, Fr. *mon père n'est pas Français.*

Cr. *Missier la cé* yon *youvênèr*, that gentleman is *a* governor, Fr. *ce monsieur est gouverneur.*

Cr. *Fouèr li cé* yon *solicitèr*, his brother is *a* solicitor, Fr. *son frère est procureur.*

It is also employed, contrary to French usage, before a noun placed in an appositive relation to another; as, *Jean ca moder doègt;* yon *baggaie moèn té save té poú river*, John is biting (his) finger (*i.e.* repenting bitterly): *a* thing I had known would come to pass, Fr. *Jean se mord le doigt (.i.e se repent amèrement): chose que j'avais su devoir se faire.*

The Indefinite Article is also used after *ça* before nouns occurring in exclamations; as, *çd* yon *zaffair!* what *a* business! Fr. *quel affaire!*

THE DEFINITE ARTICLE.

The Creole Definite Article, *la*, is appended to common nouns of both numbers and genders, when used in a specific sense; as,

Cr. *Caïe la ous montrer madame* la, *the* house you showed to *the* woman, Fr. la *maison que vous avez montrée à* la *femme.*

But it is not used, as in French, with a noun governing the possessive;* e.g. :—

Cr. *Caie papa moèn, the* house of my father, Fr. la *maison de mon père.*

Besides being employed as above, *la* comes at the end of every sentence in which there is a relative pronoun expressed or understood; as,

Cr. *Papélon la ça zôtes gaïèn* la, the sugar-loaf which you bought, Fr. *le papélon que vous avez acheté.*

Cr. *Simaïe la yeaux fair épîs zéfféts moèn* la, the dispersion they made of my things, Fr. la *dispersion qu'ils ont faite de mes éffets.*

* In fact in every case where the faintest genetive notion is involved; e.g., *pouéte Arime, the* Arima curate, *estimar fouancés, the* French steamer, *gouvênèr Labábade, the* Governor of Barbados.

The Definite Article is omitted in Creole after the preposition *nans*, in, when mentioning places familiar to both speaker and hearer, to either, or to the subject of discourse; as, *nous pas sa jouer nans savane jórdhi*, we cannot play in *the* savannah to-day, Fr. *nous ne pouvons jouer aujourd'hui dans* la *savane*.

Cr. *Sé-sé moèn aller nans pît*, my sister is gone to *the* well, Fr. *ma sœu est allée* au *puit*.

Cr. *Lhêr nous aller lacaie li, 'i té assise nans lacoû*, when we went to his house, he was sitting in *the* yard, Fr. *lorsquenous étions chez lui il était assi dans* la *cour*.

USE OF THE FRENCH DEFINITE ARTICLES.

The French Definite Article construction may be preserved in speaking of *weight*, *measure*, and *time;* as,

Cr. *Sique ca vende à cinque goûdes* li *baril*, or, *sique ca vende cinq goûdes poû yon baril*, sugar is selling at five dollars *a* barrel, Fr. *le sucre se vend à cinq gourdes* le *baril*.

Cr. *Toèle con ça-là doé yon goûde* la *yâde*, cloth like this must (be) one dollar a yard, Fr. *du drap comme ceci doit être à une gourde* le *mètre*.

Cr. *Li oní ca chanter toute* la *joûnèn*, he only sings *the* whole day, Fr. *il ne fait que chanter toute* la *journée*.

In French, to denote a portion of any sensible object or abstract quality, the partitive article *(du, de l'*, sing. mas.; *de, la, de l'*, sing. fem., and *des*, plural for both genders) is placed directly before substantives; as,

    (a) *Il mangeait* du *beurre sans pain.*
       He was eating   butter without bread.
    (b) *On a versé* de *l'encre sur mon habit.*
       They have spilt   ink   on my coat.
    (c) *La femme me donna* de la *farine.*
       The woman gave me (some) flour.

But in Creole the singular form of the partitive is never used, as may be seen in the ensuing translation :—

    (a) *'i té ca manger bêr sans pain.*
    (b) *yeaux jéter lenque la-sous habit moèn.*
    (c) *madame la ba moèn farine fouance.*

The plural partitive is sometimes used; even when in French it is replaced by the simple preposition, *de;* e.g.,

Cr. *Tiní* des *mounes qui touô bêtes,* there are persons who are too silly, Fr. *il y a des gens que sont très simples.*

Cr. *Lábbé la baîe* des *belles lives,* the priest gave (some) beautiful books, Fr. *le prêtre donna de beaux livres.*

SYNTAX OF NOUNS.

The accidents and constructions of Nouns have already been so fully discussed and illustrated above, that little remains for us here but to remark on a few points omitted, or but slightly alluded to, in our previous strictures on this class of words.

COMPOUNDED NOUNS.

It has already been seen that the Creole Possessive Case is expressed by placing the noun or pronoun denoting the owner immediately after that denoting the possession; without any other sign of the relation existing between the words so arranged. It has also been seen that the Creole construction is the French construction with case-sign *de* omitted.

This suppression of *de* is almost universal in the dialect; and gives rise to the following usages with regard to those noun-relations that are indicated in French by that preposition. A noun denoting the *material* or *species* of another, comes immediately after it, a genitive relation being implied in cases of this sort;

Creole.	*English.*	*French.*
yon cotiche bois	a sandal *of* wood	*une sandale de bois*
lamoèlle béf	ox marrow	*de la moële de bœuf*

Sometimes though in French another relation between two nouns is indicated by *à*, the Creole formula is the same ; as,

Cr. *nômme gouos ziex la*, the man *with* the large eyes, Fr. *l'homme aux gros yeux.*

This occasions ambiguities which are not possible in English or French, owing to the difference of construction employed to express the different relations above referred to ; thus,

Creole.		*English.*	*French.*
yon sac caco,	though usually,	a bag *of* cacao	*un sac* de *cacao*
	often means	a cacao-bag	*un sac* à *cacao*

To prevent mistakes, when expressions like *sac caco, boète capsiles, pañèn pain,* etc., have any but their ordinary meaning, it is usual to employ some such circumlocution as, *sac poû metter caco, boète qui té tnî capsiles, pañèn yeaux ca mette pain,* etc.

Sometimes again, the words connected by *de* or *à* are all taken together as a simple appellative,—and generally limited from a general to a particular application ; as, *louile-a-boutler* (Fr. *de l'huile à brûler,* i.e., oil to burn), lamp-oil. From the elements of this compound, it is clear that *all* oil for burning may be thus indicated ; but in Creole (at least the Trinidad Creole), it is used exclusively for *fish-oil,* and one would be thought ridiculous were he to describe pitch-oil, cocoa-nut-oil, or any other used for burning, as *louile-a-boutler.* We must, however, own that in English the same thing is observable ; for few persons (we allude to those born and bred here), ever think of any but fish-oil when *lamp-oil* is mentioned, or ever use the term except with that specific meaning.

The Creole abounds in compounded nouns, many of which it is not easy for strangers to understand ; e.g.,

Creole.	*English.*
Yon passe-pâ-tèr,	"a pass by land," i.e., one who has come from out the Bocas.
Poussèr-difé,	"shover of fire," a stirrer up of strife.
Vent-mènèn,	"wind brought," same as *passe-pâ-tèr.*
Vienti-vati, *	*(Fr. riens-tu, va-tu,)* a gadder about.
Pied-cochon,	"hog's-foot," an illusory promise.
Causer-ououge,	"red-talk," indelicate conversation.

To express "crowd," or "multitude," the Creoles employ *bâne,* (Fr. *bande)* band, or *rafale,* before the nouns denoting the objects; as, *yon* bâne *mounes té là,* a *crowd* of persons were there, Fr. *une* foule *de personnes y étaient;—li baie yon* rafale *cappars,* he gave a *great quantity* of coppers, Fr. *il a donné une quantité de sous.*

SYNTAX OF ADJECTIVES.

From what we have endeavoured to explain with regard to the Adjectives in Creole, it follows that there can be no regularity of concord between them and the nouns they qualify. The following sentences, containing as they do the current and the fortuitous forms of certain adjectives, will illustrate our doctrine: that when nouns denoting animals or inanimate objects have been adopted into Creole by themselves, adjectives qualifying them will have the form current in the dialect; but if they have been adopted in such close combination with the adjectives as to convey a single idea, the adjectives will have the form required by French usage† :—

Creole.	*English.*
Ouôbe li té faite épîs yon toèle gris, *qui té ca bien sembe* toèle-grise.	Her gown was made with (of) a *gray* cloth which very much resembled *holland.*
Ece dleau-blanche *cé yon* dleau blanc ?	Is a *white* liquid ?

* Sometimes a verb.   See List of Idioms for more of these compounds.

† Part Second, page 28.

Creole.	English.
Jôrdhi cé la-pleine-line, *et* laline plein dleau.	To-day it is *full* moon and the moon (is) *full* of water.
Moune ca crier in-pé boéssons dleaux forts, *main yeaux pas faibes passé* dleau-forte.	They call spirits "strong waters;" but they are less strong than *aquafortis*.
Medicine-douce *pas medecine qui* doux, *toujoûs*.	A black draught is not by any means a *sweet* medicine.

From the above examples it follows also that nouns denoting animals and inanimate objects have no grammatical gender.

POSITION OF ADJECTIVES.

The place of the Adjectives in Creole, as in French, is usually *after* the Noun; e.g.,

Creole.	English.
yon nômme gangan *et-pîs yon femme ziéx*-coqui.	a *showy* man and a *cock-eyed* woman.

There are certain adjectives which, when used singly, precede their nouns in French. Of these we shall notice a few, which, in Creole present some difference either as regards their usual position, or otherwise.

Cher, dear, is placed oftener *before* than after nouns denoting persons, and oftener *after* than before those denoting things; as,

Creole.	English.
"Chèr *maman moèn, pas lapeine plé-rer*, chèr *zamie nous 'ja maron nous*."	My *dear* mother, its of no use crying, our *dear* friend has already deserted us.
Voèlà yon toèle chèr: *quâte escallins poû yon yâde!*	Here is a *dear* cloth : forty cents for one yard !

Doux, sweet, never precedes its substantive, at least not as far as we have ever heard; as, *domplines* doux *li ca vende poú bonbons,* sweet dumplings which she sells for cakes.

Riche, rich, always follows its nouns; e.g., *yon moune* riche, a *rich* person.

Trisse (Fr. *triste*) sad, more often follows than precedes the noun, especially when a person is spoken of; as, *moèn ouèr tois tits gáçons* trisses *óti moèn té aller li,* I saw three *melancholy* boys where I went.

According to the French Grammar, *un grand homme* means a *great* man, and *un homme grand,* a *tall* man. In Creole only the former phrase is used, and it invariably means a *full grown* or *full aged* man; c.g., *yon* grand *nómme con ça pas té doé jouer épts ces jénesses la,* a *mature* man like that should not have played with those youths. To indicate a "great" man, the phrase "*grand téte*" is commonly employed; as, *vus té sa ouèr li té yon* grand tête, you could see he was a *great* personage.

GOVERNMENT OF THE ADJECTIVES.

Adjectives expressing *plenty,* or *scarcity, want, absence,* and others of similar import, require, in French, the preposition *de* before their regimen.

In Creole, they either take no preposition at all, or, what is more generally the case, any other than *di,* as may be seen by the ensuing illustrations:—

French.	*English.*	*Creole.*
il était plein de *bonté*	he was full *of* kindness	*'i té plein bonté*
beaucoup de *gens*	many persons	*yon pile mounes*

Capable de *le faire* in French, "is capable of doing it;" but in Creole, *capábe fair li,* the literal translation, does not mean exaactly the same thing.

Capábe, seldom used in a laudatory sense, always involves a reference to the character of its noun, while *sa* is the word employed in all cases to express ability, without any implication of censure. If we wish to say of a person with dishonest habits, that he is likely to tell an untruth, etc., we must in Creole use *capâbe;* e.g., *li cé yon bougue qui* capâbe *mentî,* he is a fellow who (is) *capable* of lying; i.e., he is just the kind of person to do so. If we spoke simply of his ability to run a mile, *capâbe* would give place to *sa :—i* sa *cououi yon mile;* but should we mean that he would run that distance for the purpose of stealing, *capâbe* must be used :—*'i* capâbe *cououi yon mile poû fair yon vôle;* he is *capable* of running a mile to commit a theft. Perhaps a more striking illustration may be found in the proper Creole translation of the English phrase: "he is quite *capable* of protecting himself," Fr. *il est très-*capable *de se protéger.* Here, no censure being intended, *capâbe* is not admissible: we must translate: *li* sa *pouend soèn corps-li bien.* Negatively, however, *capâbe* is only a stronger expression of ability than *sa;* e.g., *moèn pas sa bouanèn jambe moèn,* is the same as, *moèn pas* capâbe *bouanèn jambe moèn,* the former being "I cannot move my leg," while the latter may be understood as, "I am *wholly* incapable of moving my leg." The fluctuations of meaning observable in *capâbe* is common to most of the following adjectives, which reject or take the prepositions we have placed after them, according as they are placed before nouns or before verbs :—

French.	*English.*	*Creole.*
chargé de	laden *with*	*châgé* èvec, epîs
désolé de	disconsolate *for*	*désolé* poû
las de	weary *of, with*	*lasse* èvec, èpîs
preparé de	prepared *for, to*	*pouéparé,* poû
prête à	ready *to*	*pouète* poû
rassasié de	satiated *with*	*rassasié* épîs, èvec
tourmenté de	tormented *with*	*toûmente* épîs, èvec

In Creole, such adjectives as *obligé, lasse, rassasié, honte,* etc., may in general, take no preposition before verbs and infinitives used as nouns; e.g. :—

Creole.	English.	French.
Ous doé honte pâler con ça.	You ought to be ashamed *of* speaking so.	*Vous devez avoir honte* de *parler ainsi.*
Bêf pas ca jamain lasse poter cônes li.	The ox is never weary *of* carrying his horns.	*Le bœuf n'est jamais las* de *porter ses cornes.*
Moèn rassasié épis man-ger.	I am sick *of* eating.	*Je suis rassasié* de *manger.*

It frequently happens, however, that, in order to be understood, the French must be translated into Creole by synonomous terms. An ancient inhabitant of some country district, who has had but few opportunities of hearing, and less of learning, French, (or even what we may call the *high patois*,) would find it difficult to comprehend our meaning, if we told him, *nómme la digne di louange*, the man is worthy of praise. Doubtless, the two first words of our statement would be very plain; but all the rest might have been so much Greek, for all he should understand about it. But if we come down to his vernacular, and try, *nómme la mériter yeaux vanter li*, the man deserves (that) they (should) praise him, or, *nómme la mériter baie bon nom*, the man deserves to be given good name, it would be all clearness, all light, to our rustic friend.

The examples we have given above of the pronouns required by adjectives might be multiplied greatly; but we believe they suffice to show the points of difference, in this respect, between the dialect and the parent speech.

COMPARATIVES.

To express *than* before infinitives, the French employ *que de*, but the Creoles *passé poú* and sometimes *passé* alone; e.g. :—

Creole.	English.	French.
Li die simié zôtes té batte li passé poù *té bà 'i yon tape con*ça.	He said it is better you had beaten him *than* to have played him such a trick.	*Il dit que ce serait mieux que vous l'au-riez battu* que de *l'a-voir joué un pareil tour.*
Meièr li môr passé dri-*vaïer toûpâtout.*	It is better for him to die *than* to keep wan-dering about.	*Mieux pour lui serait de mourir* que de *ra-gabonder.*

Before any tense of the Indicative, the French express *than* by *que ne,* when the sentence is not interrogative : in Creole *passé* is the word employed in this case also. *Poú*, being an infinitive sign, is not admissible :—

Creole.	English.	French.
Ous plis mêle passé *moèn té ca coèr.*	You are more astute *than* I thought.	*Vous êtes plus fin* que *je* ne *pensais.*
I plis bon passé *ous ca die.*	He is better *than* you are saying.	*Il est meilleur* que *vous* ne *dites.*

Before numerals the Creoles generally omit *plis,* using *passé* alone in comparisons : the French *plus* requires *de* immediately before the numeral; as,

Creole.	English.	French.
Tiní passé *tois caïes lôte-bôd cela-moèn.*	There are more *than* three houses beyond mine.	*Il y a* plus de *trois maisons au-delà de la mienne.*
Li métter passé *yon douzaine mounes endidans.*	He has put in (cheated) more *than* a dozen persons.	*Il a trompé* plus d'une *douzaine de gens.*

SYNTAX OF PRONOUNS.

PERSONALS.

The place of the Personal Pronouns in the nominative case, is invariably before the verb, whatever may be the nature of the proposition ; as,

Creole.	English.
"*Moèn coucher nans sérein,* *Dos moèn tout mouïé :* *Zótes bâ moèn laclé la* *Poú m'aller changer.*"	*I* lay in the dew, My back is all wet: Do *you* give me the key That *I* may go and dress.

Creole.	English.	French.
Oti nous *yé?* ça zôtes ca boèr ?	Where are *we ?* what drink *ye ?*	*Où sommes*-nous ? *que buvez*-vous ?

In exclamatory phrases, the French often place the nominative pronouns *after* the verb, as is done in interrogatories ; but the Creole, inflexible and prosaic, allows no such latitude. Impassioned utterances must therefore conform to immutable usage, which requires the verb to always follow its nominative ; for example :—

French.	English.	Creole.
"*Soldats !*" *s'écria-t*-il, "*qui m'aime me suive !*"	"Soldiers!" exclaimed *he,* "let him that loves me follow me !"	Li *héler,* "*Soldats !*" "*ça qui aimèn moèn souive moèn !*"
Que viens-je *d'entendre !*	What have *I* just heard !	*Qui ça* moèn *sôti tende / la !*

" When there are two or more pronouns in the nominative case, a resuming pronoun, such as *nous, vous, ils,* is generally used in French as the subject of the following verb ; as,

French.	English.	Creole.
Vous et moi, nous *partirons.*	You and I will depart.	*Ous et pîs* moèn *câer pâtî.*
Vous et nous, nous *payerons.*	You and we will pay."[*]	*Zôtes épîs* nous *va payer.*

As may be seen in the foregoing illustrations, the Creole coincides with the English in having no resuming pronoun.

In imitation of French colloquial custom, the Personals are often repeated at the end of clauses or sentences, to give prominence to the individual they represent. This use of the pronouns is equivalent to the English "for my part," "as to you," etc.; thus—

* Delille's French Grammar, page 265.

Creole.	English.	French.
Zòtes die zòtɛs lasse jouer : moènpôncôr lasse, moèn.	You have said you are weary playing; I, *for my part,* am not yet weary.	*Vous dîtes que vous êtes fatigués de jouer :* je *ne le suis pas,* moi.
Li tinî lagent, li.	*As to him,* he has money.	*Il a de l'argent,* lui.

Before *pas* and *aller*, the first personal pronoun, *moèn* is usually abbreviated :—

Creole.	English.
Yeaux ca die m'pas* *vlé travaîe ;* et *lhêr* m'aller travaîe yeaux pas ca vlé payer.	They say *I* do not want to work; and when *I* go to work, they do not wish to pay.

The position of the Personal pronouns with regard to each other, when there are two or more governed by the same verb, is a very perplexing matter in French. But the Creole arrangement of these words is the same as with regard to nouns : datives immediately following the verb and accusatives after. Of course if the sentence has not a dative, the accusative is next to the verb :—

Creole.	English.	French.
Moen machicoter li. †	I chew *it.*	*Je* l'ai mâché.
Ous pas marer nous.	You did not bind *us.*	*Vous* nous *avez pas amarrés.*
Iouèr li.	He saw *it.*	*Il* le *vit.*
Moèn pâncôr die 'i li.	I have not yet told *it* to him.	*Je ne* le *lui ai pas encore dit.*
Bâ 'i li.	Give *it* to her.	*Donnez*-le *lui.*

* Pronounced : *Yo deem-pah-vlay trah-vigh,* etc.

† Bearing in mind the relation in which the first concoctors of the Creole stood towards those who supplied them with the vocabulary and general framework of their dialect, we should perceive that the difference of arrangement existing between the French and Creole pronominal accusative, though striking at first sight, is nevertheless, as respects the Creole, a servile follow-

In reply to questions, the French use *le*, *la*, etc., in agreement with the word to which the question refers; but in Creole the answer is either a simple *oui* (yes), or *non* (no), or the word together with the noun and verb are repeated; e.g. :—

French.	English.	Creole.
Est-ce là votre frère ?	Is that your brother?	*Cé fouèr ous ça ?*
Non, ce ne l'est pas.	No, it is not.	*Non ;* or *non, cé pas fouer moèn.*
Sont-ce là vos plumes?	Are those your pens?	*Ece cé plimes ous ça ?*
Oui, ce les sont.	Yes, they are.	*Oui; cé plimes moèn.*

The French pronoun *y* is sometimes represented in Creole by *la-sous ça*, on that, *la-sous li*, on it, after *penser*, *combiner*, and other verbs signifying to think or reflect; as,

Creole.	English.	French.
Ous c'aller combiner la-sous ça	You will reflect *on it*	*Vous y penserez*

En, denoting a part, and used relatively in French, is not found in Creole, except as an insignificant syllable of the hortatory words, *tempouie* (i.e. *t'-en-prie*), and *soyé-ous-en-sî (soyez-vous en sur).** The partitive sense of *en* is sometimes represented by *la-dans*, in it; e.g. :—

French.	English.	Creole.
Je n'en ai reçu que trois.	I have not received but three (*of them.*)	*Moèn pas touver passé tois* là-dans.

ing of, rather than a departure from French usage. Between two classes of men so different in nationality, race, position, no *conversation* strictly such was possible. From the ruling class the subject people received only *commands* —and having a language to frame for themselves, they fashioned it according to the model most frequently presented to them. "*Prenez*-le," "*coupez*-le," "*arrangez*-le," exemplify the kind of construction likeliest to strike the hearing of the Negroes : and it is no wonder that, with no teacher to guide and explain, they should believe this construction to be universal, while, in fact, it was only common. These considerations will, we think, assist towards determining the actual derivation of the verbs cited at page 48 as originations from the Imperative, or, with slighter probability, from the second person plural Indicative.

* Of *ensouhaite* also.

Where *en* is used personally, in the sense of "from him," "of him," and so forth, the Creole generally employ *nans lamain li*, *compte li*, in "his hand," "about him," etc. ; e.g. :—

French.	English.	Creole.
J'en ai reçu des bienfaits.	I have received benefits from him.	*Moèn ricivoèr bienfets* nans lamain li.
Nous en *parlerons.*	*We* shall speak of *him* (or it.)	*Nous caller pâler* compte li.

POSSESSIVE PRONOUNS.

In French the Possessive Pronouns are replaced by the Definite Article, when the sense of the phrase clearly indicates the possessor ; but in Creole no such substitution occurs : either the possessive must be used, or some other construction resorted to ; as,

French.	English.	Creole.
J'ai froid aux *mains.*	*My* hands are cold.	*Lamains* moèn *foètes.*
Vous avez mal à la tête.	*Your* head aches.	*Tête* ous *ca fair ous mal.*
Il a le corps trop gros et la *tête trop petite.*	*His* body is too large and *his* head too small.	*Corps* li *touop gouos, et-* *pîs tête* li *touop pitit.*
Tu lui dois la *vie.*	You owe *your* life to him.	*Oûs ca doé li lavie* ous.
Nous vînmes tous les mains liées derrière le *dos.*	We all came with *our* hands tied behind *our* backs.	*Nous toutes vinî èvec lamain* nous *marées dèïèr dos* nous.

To express "one of," as in the phrase, "one of my friends," the Creole expression is identical with the Spanish, and differs from the English and French in both of which the preposition is used :—

French & English.	Creole & Spanish.
un de *mes frères*	*yon fouèr moèn*
one *of* my brothers	*un hermano mio*

RELATIVE PRONOUNS.

For the rules that regulate the employment of the relative, *qui*, *ça*, etc., see Second Part, page 39.

DEMONSTRATIVE PRONOUNS.

Celui-ci, this one, the latter, and *celui-là*, that one, the former, are represented in Creole by *ça-là*, this one, and *lôte-là* the other one; but chiefly with reference to visible objects. The use of them in the following literal translation would be puzzling to a mere Creole:—

French.	*English.*	*Creole.*
"*L'opulence et* le *repos sont à une si grande distance l'un de l'autre que plus on approche de* celle-la, *plus on s'éloigne de* celui-ci.	Opulence and tranquility are at so great a distance from each other, that the more we approach *the former*, the more we remove from *the latter*." *	*Richesse et-pîs lavie-doux si loèn yône-à-lôte, plis nous ca vinî poués* lôte-là, *cé plis nous câller loèn* ça-là.

Instead of using *lôte-la* and *ça-là* in a statement like the above, a Creole would repeat the substantives ;—*plis nous ca vinî poués* richesse, *é plis nous ca aller loèn* lavie-doux :—or he might use *yone di yeaux* nd *lôte-là* ; which would destroy the definiteness of the statement, although without changing its meaning; for wealth and tranquility being moved from each other, it follows that approaching either is re-ling from the other :—*plis moune aller poués* yône di yêaux, *cé plis* h *quitter* lôte-là *dèïèr*, the more one approaches *one of them*, the ne he leaves *the other* behind.

ï, this or that, the French demonstrative, is used before *être*, tɑ, in the sense of *it, they*, etc., according to the number and pɛn of the verb; e.g. : *c'est moi*—*it* is I; ce *sont mes gens*—*they* any people; but in Creole the expressions *c'est* it is, and *c'était*, it w are considered as single words. They retain their demonstra-tiƴeaning only in part, and, especially *cé*, discharge the func-tiɔf the substantive verb in attributive clauses ; e.g. :—

* Delille's French Grammar.

Creole.	*English.*	*French.*
Moèn cé* *yon bon moune.*	*I am* a good person.	*Je* suis *une bonne personne.*
Ous cé *papa nous.*	You *are* our father.	*Vous* êtes *notre père.*
Li cé *gouos pague.*	He *is* a great personage.	*Il* est *un grand homme.*

PLURAL.

Nous cété* *louois.*	We *were* kings.	*Nous* étions *des rois.*
Zôtes cété *pions.* †	You *were* day-laborers.	*Vous* étiez *des laboureurs*
Yeaux cété *bons mounes.*	They *were* decent folks.	*Ils* étaient *des gens dé-* *cents.*

After the verb *ouèr*, the Creole demonstrative *çala* (as well as *là*) is added to *moèn* and *ous*, to direct particular attention to the speaker or the person addressed. *Li, nous, zôtes,* and *yeaux* usually take *là* alone, for the same purpose; e.g. :—

Creole.	*English.*	*French.*
Ous té ouèr moèn-çala *la-* *caïe ous ?*	Did you see *me* at your house ?	*M'avez-vous vu, moi* *chez vous ?*
Ous ouèr li-là, *'i bon coté* *baton li, va.* ‡	You see him there ? he is good at his stick (I can tell you.)	Le *voyez-vous ? il ë* *maître de son bat.*
Ous-çalà *bâ moèn zé-* *trenne !*	*You,* make me a Christ-mas present !	Vous, *me donner ë* *étrennes !*

When used as in the last example, *ous-ça-là* and *moèn-çalà* express incredulity, indignation, or contempt, on the part of the speaker.

---

* Not to speak of securing uniformity, (as in the case of *té, seré,* et. the abandonment of the inflected forms *c'est* and *c'était* would be desirable if were only for our being accustomed to see them exclusively in the third singular.

† Sp. *pcon.*

‡ Such interjections as *va, toujoûs, oui,* and others cannot be translated though they produce distinct impressions on the hearer's mind.

INDEFINITE PRONOUNS.

Like *on* in French, *moune* and *yeaux* are employed by Creoles to indicate in a vague and general way, *many*, *some*, and *all* persons ; e.g. :—

Creole.	English.	French.
Moune *ca die Lacotefème loèn : ça pas voué, tou-joús.*	*People* say that the Spanish Main is far : that is by no means true.	On *dit qae La Côte-ferme est loin : ce n'est pas vrai du tout.*
Yeaux *ca échouer stimar poú ranger li.*	*They* are stranding the steamer in order to repair her.	On *fait atterir le bateau-à-vapeur pour le réparer.*

After *toute-moune*, every body, *chaquin*, each one, and other distributive pronouns, the Creoles use *yeaux*, they, them, their, instead of the singular *li ;* e.g. :—

Creole.	English.	French.
Toute bête-à-fé ca clérer poú nâme yeaux.	Every glow worm sheds light for *their* (its) soul.	*Chaque bête-à-feu éclaire pour son âme.*
Toute moune ca châcher bèen poú corps-yeaux.	Every body seeks good for *themselves* (himself.)	*Chaqu'un cherche du bien pour* soi-même.

For *quiconque*, whoever, *quelconque*, whatever, the Creole eqnivalent is *quicon* which is used adjectively; e.g. :—quicon *moune ous die ça pas c'aller coèr, whoever* you tell that to will not believe ; quicon *baggaïe ous vlé,* whatever (thing) you desire.

SYNTAX OF VERBS.

VERBS WITH TWO REGIMENS·

We have already seen that when in Creole a verb has two cases, a dative and an accusative, after it, the latter must invariably come *first.*

No sign of the dative is used in Creole after the following verbs, which take in French the preposition *à* before substantives in that case :—*appouende*, to teach ; *baie*, to give ; *confier*, to entrust ; *die*, to tell ; *doé*, to owe ; *écrie*, to write ; *moutrer*, to show ; *pomette*, to promise ; *pouéter*, to lend ; *rimette, ritoûnèn*, to give back ; *sémenter*, to swear ; etc. :—

EXAMPLES.

Creole.	English.	French.
Moèn pas sa écrie papa *ous ça.*	I cannot *write* that *to* your *father.*	Je *ne puis* écrire *cela* à *votre* frère.
Madame la rimette iche *li baggaïe la.*	The lady *returned* the object *to* her *child.*	*La dame remit l'objet* à *son* enfant.
Si ous pouéter Jean *çavolant la, li c'aller baîe tit sé-s: ous cinq-sous.*	If you *lend* the kite *to* Jean, he will *give* a half-bit *to* your little sister.	*Si vous* prétez *le cerf-volant* à Jean, *il* donnera *cinq sous* à *votre petite* sœur.

GOVERNMENT OF VERBS.

There are verbs which in French require the preposition *à* or *de* before an infinitive.

In Creole, the following take no preposition, though in French they require *à* :—*accoutimèn*, to accustom ; *aimèn*, to like ; *appouende*, to teach ; *châcher*, to seek ; *habitouer*, to accustom ; *pessister*, to persist ; *pouéférer*, to prefer ; *rider*, to help ; *rinoncer*, to renounce ; *simier*, to prefer ; *vaûmier*, to prefer ; etc.

EXAMPLES.

Creole.	English.	French.
Moèn accoutimèn *corps-moèn léver nans sommeî douvant-joû.*	I have *accustomed* myself to wake at dawn.	*Je me suis accoutumé* à *me reveiller au point du jour.*
Zôtes pas aimèn rider *gens zôtes* fair *pièce travaî.*	You do not *like* to *help* one to do any work at all.	*Vous n'*aimez *pas* à *aider* (à) *vos gens* à *faire nul travail.*
Nous pas ca rinoncer *danser bellairs.*	We would not *renounce* dancing bellairs.	*Nous ne* renoncerions *pas* à *danser des bellairs.*

The following, with *à* in French, usually take *poù* in Creole before infinitives :—*balancer*, to hesitate ; *consentî*, to consent ; *encourager*, to encourage ; *engager*, to engage ; *offèr*, to offer ; *sévî*, to serve ; *travaîe*, to work ; etc.

EXAMPLES.

Creole.	English.	French.
Yon nômme qui tinî les- pouit pas ca balancer poù *fair douvoir li.*	A sensible man does not *hesitate* to do his duty.	*Un homme sensé ne* balance *pas à faire son devoir.*
Moèn consentî poù *aller ba ous.*	I *consented* to go for you.	*Je* consens à *aller pour vous.*
I té engager poù *travaîe yon mois tout-sêl.*	He had *engaged* to work for only one month.	*Il s'était* engagé à *travailler pour un mois seulement.*

The following verbs requiring *de* in French, usually take no preposition before an infinitive :—*cesser*, to cease ; *chàger*, to commission ; *coumencer*, to begin ; *conséîer*, to advise ; *consentî (poù)*, to consent ; *continouer*, to continue ; *craine*, to fear ; *défende*, to forbid ; *mander*, to ask ; *empécher*, to prevent ; *entoupouende*, to undertake ; *envie*, to long for ; *fôcer*, to force ; *honte*, to be ashamed ; *ménacer*, to threaten ; *mériter*, to deserve ; *obliger*, to compel ; *ôdonner*, to order ; *oblier*, to forget ; *pouèngàde*, to take care ; *pèr*, to dread ; *pouier*, to pray ; *rifiser*, to refuse ; *rigrétter*, to regret ; *ristier*, to risk.

EXAMPLES.

Creole.	English.	French.
Moèn (ca) craine *trapper ça moèn* mander *poù.*	I *fear* to obtain what I have asked for.	*Je* crains d'obtenir *ce que j'ai demandé.*
I pèr *métter corps-li nans tête bane la.*	He *is afraid* to place himself at the head of the band.	*Il* a peur de *se mettre à la tête de la bande.*

N

Creole.	English.	French.
Poûqui ous rifiser *aller ?*	Why have you *refused* to go?	*Pourquoi avez-vous re-fusé d'aller ?*
Moèn honte pôter ces pô-trets-ça-là.	I *am ashamed* to carry these pictures.	*J'ai* honte de *porter ces tableaux-ci.*
Gens qui ca conséïer *moune gaïèn chou-val gouos boudin, pas ca* rider *moune nourî li.*	They who *advise* one to buy a big-bellied horse, do not *help* to feed him.	*Ceux qui vous* conseil-lent *d'acheter un cheval à gros ventre, ne vous* aident *pas à le nourrir.*

The following verbs of the same class in French, are usually employed in Creole with the prepositions placed after them : *affliger* poû, afflict *for* ; *blâmer* davoèr, to blame *for* ; *convinî* poû, to agree *to* ; *délibérer* poû, to deliberate *to* ; *disconvinî* poû, to disagree *to* ; *fouémî* poû, to shudder *to* ; *offèr* poû, to offer *to* ; *sémenter* poû, to swear *to* ; *ripouocher* davoèr, *to* reproach *for* ; *tâder* poû, to delay *to* ; *texter* poû, to attempt *to* ; *trembler* poû, to tremble *to.*

EXAMPLES.

Creole.	English.	French.
I tenter poû *bâ nous yon bôte : main nous té là poû corps-nous.*	He *attempted* to cheat us ; but we were alive to our interests.	*Il* tenta de *nous tromper ; mais nous gardions nos intérêts.*
Yeaux fouémî poû *ouèr coument nômme la ristier mouter en-lair mât la.*	They *shuddered* to see how the man ventured to climb to the top of the mast.	*Ils ont* frémi de *voir comment l'homme se risquait en montant le mât.*
Li pas sa tâder poû *vinî.*	He cannot *delay* in coming.	*Il ne peut* tarder de *venir.*

The foregoing examples are intended as illustrations only of *general* usage. For the duties required of a living language are so manifold and various, that their complete fulfilment demands a vocabulary nothing less than infinite. Yet every language, however copious, is but a limited assemblage of words; and these, if restricted each one to a special signification, would be hopelessly inadequate to the vast requirements of human intercourse. Hence the necessity of multiplying constructions and applications of single terms; and hence, also, the impossibility of binding certain words to certain constructions, as may be seen by the changes of prepositions allowable in French and Creole to almost every one of the verbs we have cited above.

USE OF THE MOODS AND TENSES.

Verbs with *ca.*

INDICATIVE MOOD PRESENT TENSE.

The Present Tense is very often used in Creole, as in other idioms, to describe past occurrences with greater vividness and force. But, as it is the Present Tense of only verbs with *ca* that can be so employed, a very tiresome effect is often produced by a too frequent recurrence of that monosyllable. This a skilful speaker avoids by a judicious mingling of past tenses with the historical present, e.g. :—

Creole.	*English.*	*French.*
Con moèn ca soti *nans lapôte la, i* ca fair *moèn yon coûde baton; lhèr moèn* trapper *coup la,* etc.	As I *come* out of the door he *deals* me a blow with a stick; when I *received* the stroke, etc.	*Comme je* sortais *par la porte, il me* donna *un coup de baton;* lorsque *je* reçus *le coup, etc.*

As in French and English, the Present Tense is often employed for the Future; especially when an action shortly to take place is spoken of; e.g. :—

Creole.	*English.*	*French.*
Moèn ca vini *dèmain même.*	I *come* to-morrow.	*Je* viens *demain même.*

THE IMPERFECT TENSE.

The employment of this tense is the same in Creole as in other languages. It denotes an action going on at the occurrence of another that is past; e.g. :—

Creole.	English.	French.
Nômme la passer la-sous lanse la lhèr ces warahons la té ca haler *couïal yeaux.*	The man passed on the beach when the Warahoons (Indians) *were dragging* their canoe.	*L'homme passa sur l'anse lorsque les warahons tiraient leur courial.*

The Imperfect also denotes actions habitually or frequently done; e.g. :—

Creole.	English.	French.
Comment zôtes té ca fair *ɿéter sans pomenèn nans nouite ?*	How *did* you *manage* to dispense with taking walks at night ?	*Comment* faisiez *vous pour vous dispenser de vous promener dans la nuit ?*

Preceded by *si* (if), the Imperfect is used in relation to present time, and implies that the speaker is persuaded to the contrary of his hypothetic statement. The same usage obtains in French; as,

Creole.	English.	French.
Si moèn té ca vinî *là, moèn sé ouèr compte zaffaire la moèn-même.*	If I were in the habit of coming there, I should have looked after the business myself.	*Si je* venais *là, je verrais à ces affaires moi-même.*

After *si*, the Imperfect has sometimes the force of a conditional; e.g. :—

Creole.	*English.*	*French.*
Si ous té ca dîe *ça qui nans lîdée ous, moune sé save ça yeaux doé fair poû ous.*	If you *would tell* what is in your mind, one should know what to do for you.	*Si vous* disiez *ce que vous avez à l'esprit, on aurait su que faire pour vous.*

SUBJUNCTIVE MOOD.

In connexion with *si*, we may notice and dispose of that usage of the verb which in the paradigms we have called the Subjunctive Mood.

Its Present Tense is the same as the Past of the Indicative, with *si* or some other conjunction prefixed; e.g. :—

INDICATIVE PAST.	SUBJUNCTIVE PRESENT.
Cr. *Moèn* manger.	*Si moèn* manger.
Eng. I ate.	If I eat.
Fr. *Je* mangeai.	*Si je* mange.

The Past Subjunctive in Creole is the Pluperfect Indicative, with a conjunction prefixed; as,

INDICATIVE PLUPERFECT.	SUBJUNCTIVE MOOD.
Cr. *Moèn* té manger.	Si *moèn* té manger.
Eng. I *had eaten.*	*If* I *ate*, or had eaten.
Fr. *J'avais* mangé.	*Si* j'avais mangé.

It is evident from the above that what we have called the Subjunctive in Creole has little in common with that mood in French. The latter is an independent form and usage of the verb, totally distinct from the Indicative, while the former, that is to say, the Creole Subjunctive, is a mere variation of the Indicative construction. It would be a waste of time to write a disquisition on so barren a theme.

VERBS WITHOUT *CA*.

As has been shown,* the verbs conjugated without this auxilliary are few in number, and differ from the other verbs only in the Present and Imperfect Tenses. Their Imperfect, Preterite, Perfect, and Pluperfect are identical.

When constructed with *ca*, they express an habitual action or state of mind contingent on and resulting from another ; e.g. :—*Moèn* häî *mounes qui méprisants*, I *hate* disdainful people (as a present existing sentiment) :—*moèn* ca häî *mounes lhér yeaux ca jair bétise épîs corps li*, It *is my custom to hate* persons when they make fools of themselves. *Yeaux* honte *mander nous ça*, they *are* (at this present moment) *ashamed* to ask us that ; *yeaux* ca honte *mander poû* ça *yeaux bisoèn*, They *are* (habitually) *ashamed* (whenever they are) to ask for what they require. From which examples it will be seen that the distinction between the conjugations is not a matter of mere fancy, but a fact of some importance.

Sometimes the meaning given to the verbs by the addition of *ca* is inceptive, and denotes the beginning of a mental feeling or condition ; as, *moèn* ca aimèn *place la*, I *am getting fond* of the place ; *yeaux* ca honte *gens ycaux, apouésent*, they *are growing* ashamed of their people, now.

THE PRESENT AND PAST PERFFCT TENSES.

The Present Perfect Tense of verbs conjugated with *ca* is simply the Infinitive placed after a nominative case ; as *chêper*, to excel greatly, *li* chêper *nous*, he *has* greatly *excelled* us.

The Past Perfect is formed by prefixing *té* to the foregoing tense ; as, *li té* chêper *nous*, he *had* greatly *excelled* us.

As the Preterite and Perfect meanings of a verb are not indicated by any difference of construction, it is sometimes found necessary to employ, as a perfect sign, *jà*, an abbreviation *of déjà*, already ; e.g., *li ja casser toutes zassiettes la* déjà, *qui lapeine boûgonnèn ?* he

---

* Part Second, page 60.

has *broken* all the plates *already*, what is the use of grumbling? We are aware that *jà* does ordinarily mean the same as *déja*; but in the simultaneous use of them, as in the foregoing sentence, there is something deeper than the seeming tautology.

THE INFINITIVE MOOD.

Every infinitive in Creole is used as a substantive. This license has given rise to a variety of singular constructions. Commonest among these is the repetition of the infinitive with a possessive pronoun, as a complement to some other mood of the same verb; e.g. : dômî dômî *ous*, "*sleep* your *sleep*," i.e., *go on sleeping; moèn* coucher coucher *moèn, lhèr moèn tende battaïe là*, "I *lay* my *lying* when I heard the fight; i.e., I *remained lying* when I heard the fight;— tempoüie, léssez-nous sôtî sôtî nous*, "Pray, let us *go out* our *going out;*" i.e., allow us *to carry out* our intention of *going out*. In this way a variety of impressions is conveyed; but the cardinal notion underlying them all, is the continuance or prosecution of an inchoate state or action.

Besides their employment as above illustrated, the infinitives supply the place of participles.

PARTICIPLES.

Especially in verbs ending in *er*, the Creoles present participial termination is *ant;* as, *mangeant, dansant*, eating, dancing. But generally speaking, the use of this mood is very limited. Verbs ending otherwise than in *er* have generally no participial form; as, *coude*, to sew, *répône*, to answer. This defect it is attempted to remedy in the following ways: the preposition *en* is placed before the verb; e.g., en coude *yon moceau la-sous lôte, ous ca gáter ces toèles la*, by *sewing* one piece on the other you are spoiling the cloths.

Sometimes *ca* is placed before the Verb; e.g. :—

Creole.	*English.*
Ca dïe *yon baggaïe*, ca ridîc *yon baggaïe tous-lé-mouments, ca embéter moèn*.	*Saying* and *repeating* a thing every minute, bothers me.

Con (Fr. comme), as, placed before *ca*, also gives the verb a participial sense ; e.g. :—

Creole.	*English.*

Con *canôte la* ca boucler *poènte la, gâdez comment li belle !*	See how beautiful the boat looks, as it is *rounding* the point !

The simple infinitive may sometimes have the force of a present participle ; e.g. :—

Creole.	*English.*

Moén save batte *yon mammaïe poú toute tit baggaïe pas ca fair li bon.*	I know that *beating* a child for every little fault does not make him good.

On the whole, it would appear that present participial constructions, pure and simple, are not much favoured in Creole.

PAST PARTICIPLES.

Verbs in *er* may be credited with a past participle whenever it may be found necessary in Creole ; thus, *'i té* assiré *ça*, he was *assured* of that ;—*nous rester bien* coupés, " we remained well *cut ;* i.e., we were thoroughly *disappointed.* But, as has been already observed, (p. 63,) these past participles retain but little, if any, verbal energy ; having subsided into mere adjectives. Altogether, this is a most difficult point, the complete investigation of which requires more time and research than we can devote to it. The following facts, however, may be noticed in connexion therewith.

Few French verbs whose past participles end in sounds different from that of their infinitives, have past participles in Creole. Consequently, if we frame a passive construction having an instrumental case, (governed by *par*,) the infinitive must be employed ; e.g., *jilet moèn té* coude *pá yon bon täïèr*, my waistcoat was *sewn* by a good tailor. If we use the French *cousu* instead of *coude*, no mere Creole would understand us. But, besides the probability of being misunderstood, if too Frenchified in his *patois*, an affected speaker incurs the certainty of being ridiculed for his pains. Whosoever condescends to talk Creole, must, for the while, forget his French, and believe (for it is a fact) that he is using a dialect fully capable of expressing all ordinary thoughts, provided the speaker is master of, and understands how to manage, its resources.

IDIOMATIC CONJUGATIONS.

To express the *act of doing*, or *being on the point of doing*, in time past or present, infinitives are, in Creole, constructed as follows:—

Cé or *cété* is placed before them, and a nominative case with some other mood of the same verb after; as,

Creole.	English.
Cé gàder *moèn* ca gàder ça.	I am *just looking* at that.
Cété gàder *moèn* té ca gàder.	I *was* in the *act of looking*.

To denote an intention on the point of being carried out, *aller* is employed; as;

Cé aller *li té* ca aller *bâ moèn dleau la*.	He *was just about to* give me the water.
Cé aller *li* cáller *die* ça.	He *is on the point of* saying so.

To intimate that an action has just been done, *sóti*, to come out from, is used with the verb, as in the following examples:—

Creole.	English.	French.
Moèn sóti *contrer épis yon moune moèn pas té soucier ouèr.*	I have *just* met one whom I had but little desire of seeing.	*Je* viens de *rencontrer quelqu'un que je n'avais pas un grand désir de voir.*

A repetition of *sóti*, adds force to the idea of recentness; e.g.:—

Cé sóti *yeaux* sóti *manger: pas bâ yeaux pièce encor.*	They have been eating but this instant: don't give them a bit more.	*Ils* viennent de *manger: ne leur donnez rien de plus.*

ADDITIONAL REMARKS ON A FEW VERBS.

Fr. *Avoir*,   To Have; *Etre*, To Be.
Cr. *Tinî*,

The place of *avoir*, as a principal verb, is filled in Creole by *tinî*, while as an auxilliary it has been displaced, as we have seen, by different parts of *étre*.

With regard to *tinî*, it is curious to observe how it has supplanted *avoir*, not only in ordinary phraseology, where the primary import of both,—namely, *possession*—suggests and explains the substitution, but also in some of those idioms in which the possessive notion is by no means so prominent. Not less singular is the coincidence of Creole with Spanish, and other Romance dialects, in preferring *tenir* to *avoir* in possessive and other analogous constructions. We subjoin examples, with Spanish equivalents :—

French & English.	*Creole & Spanish.*
*J'*ai *un* *tres-joli* *livre.*	*Moèn* tinî *yon bien belle* *live.*
I *have* a very handsome book.	*Yo* tengo *un* *muy hermoso libro.*
Il avait *de l'argent.*	*Li* té-tinî *lâgent.*
He *had* money.	*El* tenia *dinero.*
Nous avions *raison.*	*Nous* té-tinî *réson.*
We were in the right.	*Nosotros* teníamos *razon.*
*N'*ayez *pas peur.*	*Pas* tinî *pèr.*
Be not afraid.	*No* tenga *cuidado.*

The French construction *d'avoir* (as after *blâmer*, *accuser*, etc., where *d'avoir* signifies *for having*, *with having*, etc.,) is in Creole a pure conjunction; viz., *davoèr*. This word, like other conjunctions derived from verbs, retains much of its radical import, though, of course, deflected and obscured; as,

Creole.	*English.*
Papa moèn bîmèn moèn davoèr *moèn pas té vlé fair ça 'i dîe moèn.*	My father beat me, *because* I did not want to do what he told me.

Another part of *avoir* found in Creole, is *aura*, employed as in French to express probability or likelihood; as,

| Creole. | English. |

Li aura *viní lacaîe lhêr nous té nans léglise.* He *must have* come to our house when we were in church.

The third person singular Indicative Present of *avoir;* viz., *a*, is found in the Creole phrase *napoènt* (i.e., *n'a point*) which means, "there is no," "there was no;" as,

" *Celesse Sainte Anne, O!*
Si napoènt *tambouïer,*
N'a virer."

Celeste of St. Anne's!
If *there is no* drummer,
We shall return.

Yeaux châcher couteau, napoènt *couteau.* We searched for a knife, *there was* no knife (to be found.)

The infinitive of the French verb *to be* is but rarely used in Creole; no substantive verb being ever expressed in attributive propositions relating to present time.

Etant, the present participle, is a Creole conjunction meaning, *inasmuch as, since,* etc.; as,

Camarades zôtes étant *té là, poûqui zyeaux pas bäïe zôtes lamain ?* Since your companions were present, why did they not aid you?

Est, pronounced in Creole *yest,* serves in particular cases, through all the persons of the Present Indicative of the verb.—See page 78.

Concerning the other parts of *étre* commonly used in Creole, see Auxilliaries pp. 50—52.

SYNTAX OF ADVERBS.

Adverbs, as a general rule, come *after* the word they qualify; as,

Creole.	*English.*
Yeaux ca vinî dri.	They come *often.*
Moèn sé ja aller belle-drive.	I would have gone *long since.*
Yon tit gâçon coû à-coté.	A boy with his neck *awry.*

When used interrogatively, the Adverb commonly begins the sentence, as in other languages ; e.g. :—

Main, jisse ôti *zôtes ca mènèn nous ?*	But, *how far* are you leading us ?
Coument *zôtes sé vlé nous mouter yon cêtain mône con-ça !*	*How* could you wish us to go up a vast mountain like that ?

Adverbs of Manner present no peculiarity save in very few exceptional cases.   The following are purely native formations :—

Li fair caïe la tout cabà-cabà, *con si cé pas té lâgent yeaux té ca bâ li poû travâî li.*	He built the house quite *clumsily,* as if it was not money they were giving him for his labour.
Yeaux bâ li coups jisse temps boudins yeaux pleins; apoués, yeaux assise à-dadà *la-sous li.*	They gave him blows (beat him) till their bellies were filled (they were satisfied); after that, they sat *astride* on him.
Chein la ca mâcher cañan-cañan ; *pôr bête, zangaïle tomber abord li !*	The dog walks *painfully slow :* poor brute, evil days have overtaken him !
Pas lapeine gâder moèn en-bêne en-bêne *con-ça ; moèn va finî pièce la ba ous* au-biɢoule.	It is useless to watch me thus *furtively :* I shall finish the piece for you *in a masterly manner.*

COMPARISON OF ADVERBS.

In Creole Adverbs are usually compared, like Adjectives, by *plis,* more, or *moènce,* less, placed before them ; e.g., plis *doucement, more* softly ; *moènce long-temps,* a *shorter* while since.

As in the case of Adjectives also, the most favoured mode of expressing absoluteness of the notion conveyed by the Adverbs, is by iteration; as, *moèn pas vlé ça* pièce, *pièce,* I do not *by any means* want that ; *li vinî tout* bosale, *bosale,* he came *in the rudest possible* manner.

SYNTAX OF PREPOSITIONS.

The Creole Prepositions, as may have been seen, (p. 70.) are, in general, corruptions or compoundings of French prepositions or adverbs. We shall content ourselves with noticing one or two that present features worth noting :—

Ba or baï—poû, for.

That these two prepositions are not always exchangeable, may be seen in the following examples :—

Creole.	*English.*
Ous vlé gañèn yon chapeau ba *moèn ?*	Do you wish to buy a hat *for* me? (i.e., to save me the trouble of going myself.)
Tempouie gañèn yon chapeau poû *moèn.*	Pray buy me a hat *for* (my use.)
Yeaux ca fair bonbon la ba *moèn, pâce cé moèn qui loûer yeaux, main cè pas* poû *moèn, pisse cé pas moèn qui câller manger li.*	They are making the cake *for* me, because I hired them; but it is not *for* me (my use), since it is not I who am to eat it.

Nans, in.

After such verbs as *sôtí, tirer,* etc., this preposition means *from* or *out of* in Creole; as,

Nous pas sotî nans *bois.*	We are not come *from* the woods.
Qui moune câller tirer moèn nans *horrôpe çalà?*	Who will take me *out of* this scrape?

Epîs—evèc, with.

We may be wrong, but our impression certainly is that *epîs* is more often used among us than *evèc.* Both of them, besides serving to unite words, often denote the instrument or means; as,

Li taller lôte la à-tèr épîs *yon coûdc bouique.*	He felled the other to the ground *by* a blow with a brick.
Moèn natter ça evèc *lamains moèn.*	I plaited that *with* my hands.

La-sous—en-lair, upon.

These are every day used convertibly ; e g. :—

Creole.	English.
Tit gâçon la la-sous *dos yon gouosc hou-val,* or, *Li* en-lair *dos yon,* etc.	The boy is *on* the back of a big horse.

But there seems to be some difference between them after all, as for example in,

La-sous *tête moèn.*	*On* my head (on the-side, back.)
En-lair *tête moèn.*	*On* my head (on the crown, above.)
Li la-sous *pied-bois* la, *main li pas* en-lair *li.*	He is *on* the tree, but not *on top of* it.

SYNTAX OF CONJUNCTIONS.

As a general rule, Conjunctions are but sparingly used in Creole. In the following lines, for example, there is none, and none is needed, as the meaning is perfectly clear. But it would not be easy to translate them correctly into English or French without connectives of some sort :—

" *Femmes tombées, lever*	*Though* women fall *and* rise
Sept fois nans lavie :	Seven times in their lives,
Antoènette tomber,	*Yet* Antoinette has fallen,
Li pas sa lever !"	*And* cannot rise again !

We proceed to illustrate the use of some conjunctions :—

Ainsi—so, therefore.

Moèn 'ja dîe cé poû ous aller, ainsi *cé pas lapeine douboute là.*	I have already said you are to go ; so it is useless standing there.

Avant—rather than.

" Avant *moèn coèr*	*Rather than* think
M'a sêvî béqués,	I'd serve the whites,
M'a piler tèr	I shall tread the earth
Grand-chimin la	Of the broad road
En-bas pieds moèn."	Beneath my feet.

Mágré, si—however, if.

<table>
<tr><td>*Creole.*</td><td>*English.*</td></tr>
</table>

O*us doé aller, moncher;* magré, si ous raûmler *assise là, assise assise ous.*

You ought to go, my friend; *however, if* you prefer sitting there, sit on.

Soet, obèn—either, or.

Li pas die zôtes dex; li die soet *yone* obèn *lôte.*

He did not say you two; he said *either* one *or* the other.

None, then.

This word which is, properly speaking, an interjective particle in Creole, represents the French *donc,* by the same change of *d* into *n,* as appears in *nans* for *dans.* It comes at the end of most affirmative phrases; especially those that convey a consequential or resultive import; in fact, just like its original, *donc,* and the English *then;* e.g. :—

Li vlé goûmèn?

Does he wish to fight?

Eh-bèn quittez-li goûmèn, nonc.

Well, let him fight, *then.*

Poûtant, yet.

Yeaux sementer dié diâbe, yeaux té là, et moèn pas té ouèr yeaux, poûtant.

They swore by everything sacred, that they were there, *yet* I did not see them.

INTERJECTIONS.

As these are not significant words, they are not subject to rules of construction. But the ensuing interjectional particles deserve notice, as they are of constant occurrence in Creole discourse :—*ein hein,* or *oun houn,* yes; *ein ein* or *oun oun,* no; and the expletives, *non,* no, *oui,* yes, which come respectively at the end of negative and affirmative declarations, and impart a certain admonitory emphasis to what is said; as,

Creole.	*English.*

C'é pas poû ous riní, non.　　You must *not* come (mind you.)

Cé poû ous riní, oui.　　You *must* come (do you hear?).

Toujoús occurs at the end of affirmations in which a strong, and, in general, a hostile opinion is expressed ; as,

Cé yon baggaïe moèn bien häï, toujoûs.　　It is a thing I utterly detest.

It also intensifies a negative ; as,

Pas moèn li 'a touver nans lair li, toujoûs.　　It would not be me he will find in his way.

PART IV

INTERPRETATION—IDIOMS.

We have now ended the Grammar proper of the Creole *patois*. The composition of its vocabulary as a whole, the accidents of its individual words, and their arrangement into sentences, have all been discussed with more or less minuteness. It is now our purpose to treat, in a few brief paragraphs, of the meaning of words, both individually and in specific constructions. In doing this, we are sensible of exceeding, in some points, the limits of our present undertaking, which is a grammar, and not a dictionary. But, considering the peculiar nature of the subject, and the fact that there is, as yet, no work devoted to the exposition of the patois—of this Island at least—we anticipate the ready forgiveness of the reader, and promise that the indulgence granted will not be abused.

In order that some notion may be formed of the divergence of the Creole from the French with regard to the import and use of individual words, we shall give a few specimens of French words with meaning deflected, contracted, or diverted to totally different applications; and of French words with their ordinary Creole equivalents.

I.—FRENCH WORDS IN THEIR USUAL CREOLE ACCEPTATION.

French.	*Creole.*
Abîmer, v. to destroy, ruin, etc.	*Bîmèn*, to beat severely.
Acajou, mahogany.	*Cajou*, cedar.

French.	*Creole.*
Achat, s. a purchase.	*Achat* id.*—any transaction.
Aplanir, v. to make plain, to level.	*Planî*, to swoop down (of birds.)
Aligner, v. to put in or according to a line.	*Aliñer-corps*, to put one's-self on a level with.
Anéantir, v. to annihilate.	*Anéantî*, to worry out, to ill-treat.
Bagage, s. luggage, baggage.	*Baggaïe*, id.—thing, object.
Balloter, v. to ballot.	*Balloter*, to sway to and fro, to stagger, to dawdle.
Bamboche, s. a dwarf.	*Bamboche*, dissipation, revelry.
Bananier, s. a large rose.	*Bananièr*, a plantain-garden.
Bombe, s. bomb.	*Bombe*, a beaver hat.
Botté, part. booted.	*Botté* id. (rarely)—to be violently in love.
Bout, s. end.	*Bout(e)* id.—cigar.
Brigand, s. brigand, robber.	*Bouigand*, a pugnacious blackguard, a dissolute fellow.
Brigandage, s. robbery, etc.	*Bouigandaïe*, uproar, dissipation.
Cabane, s. cabin, hut.	*Cabane*, bed.
Camisole, s. waistcoat, jacket.	*Camisole*, jacket.
Camouflet, s. a lighted paper held under one's nose, an affront.	*Camouflet*, a back-handed slap.
Capon, s. a sharper.	*Capon*, a coward.
Capote, s. a riding-hood.	*Capôte*, a bonnet.
Carrefour, s. cross-road.	*Callefoû*, hut, hole, obscure corner.
Case, s. small house, hut.	*Caïe*, house, residence.
Casuel, adj. casual, accidental.	*Casouel*, s. perquisites.
Chaudière, s. cauldron.	*Chôdièr*, iron pot, copper.
Chicoter, v. to quarrel about trifles.	*Chicoter,* *Chipoter,* } to pester, to worry.
Commerce, s. commerce, traffic.	*Commêce* id.—mess, confusion.
Crier, v. to bawl out.	*Crier*, to call, to name.
Crise, s. crisis.	*Crise*, a fit, hysterics.
Courage, s. courage, fortitude.	*Courage*, endurance, effrontery.
Décapiter, v. to cut off the head.	*Décapiter*, to slander.

* This contraction coming after a word signifies that it sometimes has in Creole the same import as in French.

French.	*Creole.*
Ecraser, v. to crush in pieces.	*Ecraser*, to depreciate, to cast a slur upon.
Fricasser, v. to fricassee.	*Fouicasser*, id.—to fling down violently, to give angrily.
Mal-à-propos, adv. unseasonably, untoward.	*Malapouopos*, causelessly.
*Marchand,e,*s. a dealer, shop-keeper.	*Mâchâne*, a hawker about of vendibles.
Jappe, s. prattling.	*Jappe*, manner of barking; a bark.
Jurer, v. to swear, blaspheme.	*Jirer*, to curse, to abuse.
Jurement, s. an oath, blasphemy.	*Jîement*, abuse.
Père, s. father.	*Pèr*, priest.

II.—FRENCH WORDS WITH THEIR ORDINARY CREOLE EQUIVALENTS.

Almost all the sentences in this book illustrate the fact that the Creole, like all dialects of synthetic languages, is essentially analyctical. A vast number of words common in French not being used in the *patois*, it is often necessary to recur to those which are current and convey the same general notion in both idioms :—

French. English. Creole.

Aboyer, to bark —*japper*.
Aiguisé, sharp—*filé*.
Aimable, aimable—*mériter aimèn*.
Avare, avaricious—*safe poû lâgent, chice*.
Bienveillant, benevolent, *qui tinî bon* cHèr.
Démarche, gait—*mâche, game mâcher*.
Dessein, design—*ça yon moune compter fair*.
Donner, to give—*bâïe*.
Etage, story—*grinèn*.
Evidemment, evidently—*claîment*.
S'habiller, to dress—*changer*.
Hideux, hideous— *bien laide*.
Impartial, impartial —*ni poû yone ni poû lôte, jisse*.

French.	English.	Creole.

Inexorable, inexorable—*qui tini* CHèr *fer, sans pitié.*
Lit, bedstead—*couche.*
Mur, wall—*maçonne.*
Parapluie, umbrella—*parasol.*
Parer, to adorn—*fair belle.*
Plafond, ceiling—*ciel caïe.*
Porte cochère, gate—*bâïer.*
Recompenser, reward—*payer poû lapeine.*
Se reconcilier, to be reconciled—*fair zamis.*
Se réveiller, to wake—*léver nans domî.*
Taie d'oreiller, pillow-case—*sac zorïer.*
Tableaux, pictures—*portréts.*
Toit, roof—*combe.*
Des vitres, window panes—*glaces finêtcs.*

IDIOMS.

Idioms are modes of expression peculiar to a language, and which if literally rendered into another, will not give the right meaning. In Creole the number of idiomatic expressions is very large ; and, sometimes, owing to the extreme fancifulness of many of them, most difficult of interpretation. The following are samples of these singular locutions :—

Creole.	Literal.	Meaning.
Bäie lelemis laite poû boèr la-sous tête ous.	Give enemies milk to drink on your head.	*To act so as to justify their worst imputations.*
Bäïc coûde ouôche, et-pîs dïe cé laboue.	To hit with a stone, and then say it is with mud.	*To insult under pretence of jesting.*
Bäïc yon moune Bondié sans confesser.	To give a person God without confession.	*To repose unlimited confidence in him.*
Bârer lair yon moune.	To stop up a person's room.	*To cut him short.*

Creole.	Literal.	Meaning.
Batte bouche compte yon baggaïe.	To beat the mouth about a thing.	To talk incessantly, to babble, to boast, about a thing.
Batte tamboû et-pîs danser li.	To beat a drum and dance it.	To flatly contradict one's own previous statements.
Bouef la-sous yon causer.	Brief on a discourse.	To stop short in a discourse.
Châgez waïà ous, moncher.	Load your hamper, my friend.	Take a long swill at the bottle.
Nômme la tinî yon tit cochon ca nourî poû ous.	That man has a pig feeding for you.	He owes you a grudge.
Li casser bois nans zoreîes li.	He broke wood in his ears.	He turned a deaf ear to.
Li craser toutes membes moèn.	He smashed all my members.	He moved me to deep commiseration.
Coui con dos, dos con coui.	Calabash like back, back like calabash.	Utterly disappointed in one's expectations; destitute.
Cé yon couteau phêmacie.	He is an apothecary's knife.	A man with two faces.
Chauffer dêièr zoreîe yon moune.	To warm behind a person's ear.	To incite or urge him to some deed.
Souffler zoreîe li.	To blow his ears.	To give him private warning or information.
Danser con tamboû ca batte.	To dance as the drum beats.	To accommodate one's self to prevailing customs.
Décapiter yon moune.	To decapitate a person.	To slander him without stint.
Employé lacaïe Flanigan (i.e. ca flanner.)	Employed at Flanigan's.	To be out of employ.
Entrer nans vente yon moune.	To get into a person's belly.	To cheat him out and out.
Fair "riviens-hélas."	To make return alas.	To take up again what had been abandoned.
Fair gouos magcôles.	To make large dewlaps.	To give one's self airs.

Creole.	Literal.	Meaning.
Fair yon moune mal.	To do a person harm.	*To injure him by means of witchcraft.*
Li fourer doègt nans zièx moèn.	He poked his finger into my eye.	*He presumed on my good nature to insult me grossly.*
Gens qui ca mañèn zêbes.	People who handle grasses.	*Persons addicted to* obeah.
Gâder moune à-cote.	To watch a person aside.	*To mistrust or suspect a person.*
Gañèn la-sous lespouit nous.	To gain on our sense.	*To persuade us to our disadvantage.*
Gazouïer nans päouôles li.	To babble in his talk.	*To be random, incoherent, wandering, in one's speech.*
Gens qui tinî poèles raides.	People who have stiff bristles.	*Pugnacious, stubborn people.*
Pas moèn câller haler piquant çalà épîs zôtes.	Not I will pull this thorn with you.	*I decline to discuss (or to dispute on) this matter with you.*
Lapeau ziex yeaux bien raides.	Their eyelids are very stiff.	*They are utterly ignorant of reading and writing.*
Yeaux doé lasses laver lamains la-sous zôtes.	They ought to be weary washing hands on you.	*They should be weary of beating you so often.*
Léver boucan dé'ièr mounes.	To raise a bonfire behind persons.	*To reprimand them noisily.*
Mârer yon moune.	To tie a person.	*To cast an obeah spell over him.*
Mârer vente poû yon baygaie.	To tie the belly for a thing.	*To endure every privation, strain every faculty, for its attainment.*
Mâter yon moune.	To put a mast on some one.	*To lift him suddenly off his feet.*
Li métter dleau nans ziex famîe li.	He put water in the eyes of his relations.	*He occasioned them grief.*
Ous va moder doègt lhér li touop tâd.	You shall bite finger when it is too late.	*You shall bitterly repent, etc.*

Creole.	Literal.	Meaning.
Yeaux péser la-sous laqué li.	They have pressed on his tail.	They have fined or charged him heavily.
Piéter yon moune poŭ yon baggaie.	To wait for a person with the determination of extorting satisfaction of some kind from him.	
Li tiní yon plomb.	He has a lead.	He is tipsy.
Pouend dithé poŭ la-fiève yon moune.	To take tea for some one's fever.	To interest one's self in a business more zealously than those it really concerns : to take the least notice of an individual.
Quitter chein manger yon moune.	To let dogs eat a person.	To allow every one that lists to oppress him.
Moèn pende chapeau moèn ôti lamain moèn té sa river.	I hang up my hat where my hand could reach.	I went according to my abilities, or affordings.
Pousser zaîle zoies.	To shove goose wing.	To handle a pen : to write rapidly.
Sans coucou sans graine-dor.	Without (bored) calabash, without gold bead.	Without kith or kin : utterly destitute.
Sauter baï mounes qui ca bâ li bon bouche.	To jump give persons who are giving him good mouth.	To be impetuously insolent towards those who address him with civility.
Pas sêvî pessone lampion.	Don't serve as a lamp to any body.	Do not hang on his skirts, dog his steps, be a parasite.
Yon nômme simpe.	A simple man.	A man ignorant of witchcraft; having no obeah charms, etc., wearing.
Gens qui tini zoreíes yeaux plis hauts passé têtes yeaux.	People who have their ears above their heads.	Insubordinate persons.

Creole.	*Literal.*	*Meaning.*
Tiñî poû la hènte et la golète.	Sp. Tener por la gente y la goleta.	*To have in super-abundance.*
Cé yon jêne gens qui tinî lestomac fvète.	He is a young fellow with a cold stomach.	*He cannot keep a secret; he must bring it up and out.*
Toute moune métter lamain nans bouche.	Everybody put hand to mouth.	*Every body was speechless with surprise.*
Vères qui en dèî poû gangane yeaux.	Glasses in mourning for their grandmother.	*Extremely dirty glasses.*

CREOLE PROVERBS.

Besides their value as compendious expressions of human wisdom and experience, proverbs possess the recommendation of affording, to some extent, an insight into the mental habits and capabilities of the people who invent them. It is from this latter point of view that we should have invited the reader's attention to the beautiful sayings which form the ornament of African discourse; but neither our space nor our present limited knowledge will allow our writing a formal dissertation on the subject. We trust, however, to be able to do so at some future period.

The following selection is from that vast and valuable fund of proverbial wisdom, which has been the instruction and delight of the Negro race in all ages and stages of its existence. To us, they appear admirable. We prize them as beautiful no less than intelligent deductions from the teachings of Nature, that free, infallible, and sublime volume, which Providence has displayed to all men, but more distinctly to those who have no other revelation and guidance. We certainly do not mean, that, even among the few we shall cite, there may not be some which are mere translations of French, English, or Spanish originals. On the contrary, we have been much hampered in our choice by the ever-present consciousness of the extreme difficulty of fixing the birth-place of a saying, especially when we find its parallel in so many different languages. Nevertheless, after deducting from our proverbs those of whose foreign extraction the acute reader is certain, enough will yet remain to prove that the Africans are not, after all, the dolts and intellectual sucklings that some would have the world believe them. The predominant characteristic of our proverbs is their figurativeness. Everything in Nature symbolises to the Negro something in man or man's affairs; and these applications are usually so truthful and ingenious that they are worth volumes of comments and laboured definitions. Not seldom a jingle of rhyme or a rhythmical arrangement adds to their piquancy. But the unlaboured proverb is, generally, the truest and most significant. In the ensuing selection, there are some sayings which are not current here : these are marked with asterisks.

Creole.   *English.*

Bêf pas jamain ca dîe savane, "mêci."   Ox never tells the pasture, "thank you."

This proverb alludes to the scant gratitude commonly shown to benefactors by those most indebted to them. It means also that men have little claim to acknowledgment when their good deeds have been the result of pure accident, and not of spontaneous liberality.

Pas fôte langue qui fair bêf pas sa pâler.   It is not for want of tongue that an ox cannot speak.

Men with great advantages are not always gifted with ability to improve them.

  * *Toute bois cé bois ;*   All wood is wood,
      Main mapou   Yet mapou (a worthless wood)
      Pas cajou.   Is not cedar.

Bon-temps pas bosco.   Ease is not hunch-backed.

Boudin pas tinî zoreîes.   The belly has no ears.

No train of reasoning, however exquisite, can appease the cravings of hunger.

Creole.	*English.*
Bon-bouche ca gañèn chourals à-crédit.	Fair words buy horses on credit.
Même baton qui batte chein noèr la pé batte chein blanc la.	The same stick that beat the black dog can beat the white.
Canari vlé rîe chôdièr.	The clay-pot wishes to laugh at the iron-pot.
Ous pôncor travesser läïvièr, pas jirez maman caïman.	You have not yet crossed the river, do not curse the crocodile's mother.

As Mungo Park, in his "Travels," has truly observed, the deadliest affront that can be offered to a Negro, is to abuse his mother. This proverb, therefore, means that men should beware of unpardonably offending those into whose power they possibly may fall.

Si crapaud die ous caïman tini mal-ziex, coèr-li.	If the frog tells you the crocodile has sore eyes, believe him.

In the testimony of one man concerning another, his neighbourhood and similarity of habits and living should be allowed great weight.

Cé langue crapaud qui ca trahi crapaud.	It is the frog's own tongue that betrays him.

But for the clamourous self-proclamation of some mortals, they might have lived through a life, the obscurity of which alone could save them from the world's contempt.

Crapaud pas tini chimise, ous vlé li poter cancçon!	Frog has no shirt, (the necessary,) and you wish him to wear drawers (the superfluous)!
Cououî pas laide, temps lafôce pas là.	To run away is not ugly, when one has no strength.

Discretion is the best part of valour.

Creole.	English.
Couyenade cé pas limonade.	Nonsense is not sugar-water.
Crabe pas mâcher, li pas gras ; li ma-cher touop, et li tomber nans chô-dièr.	Crab has not walked, he is not fat ; he has walked too much, and has fallen into the pot.

A judicious activity is here inculcated.

| *Déïer chein, cé " chein ;"*
Douvant chein,
Cé " missier chein." | Behind dog's back, it is " dog ;"
But before dog,
It is " mister dog." |

We take more liberties with men in their absence than when they are present.

| *Gens qui cabá ous conseï gañèn chouval gouos boudins nans lhouvênaïe, nans carême pas ca rider ous nourî li.* | They who advise you to buy a big-paunched horse in the rainy season (when grass is abundant) don't help you to feed him in the dry season (when grass is scarce.) |
| * *Si coulève pas té fonté, femmes sé pouend li fair ribans jipes.* | If the adder were not so brazen (dan-gerous) women would take it for coat-strings. |

But for the spirit of resistance known to be dormant in even the quietest of men, the freaks of tyranny would go to greater lengths.

Causer cé manger zoreïes.	Conversation is the food of the ear.
Manger yon fois pas ca riser dents.	Eating once does not wear out teeth.
Dents pas jamain ríe bons baggaïes.	Teeth never laugh at things that are good.
Dents pas ca poter dëï.	Teeth do not wear mourning.
Dents pas chérs.	Teeth are not hearts.

Innocence or lightness of heart must not always be inferred from displays of the teeth in laughter.

Creole.	*English.*

Yon doègt pas sa pouend pices. A single finger cannot catch fleas.

Doucement doète. Slow and straight.

Gens féñants ca mander travāï épîs bouche, main CHÊrs *yeaux ca pouier Bondiè poû yeaux pas touver.* Lazy people ask for work with their lips, but their hearts beg God to prevent their getting it.

Fair poû fair pas mal. Do for do is not hard.

To requite evil for evil is an easy task.

Gens bon-temps ca aller die gouvêner bonjoû. Idle people go to wish the governor good day.

Nothing is too absurd for the doing of those with nothing to do.

*La*Gêr *vêti pas ca pouend viéx nègues nans cabarets.* A war that is threatened does not overtake old negroes in the grog-shop.

Forewarned is forearmed. We can provide against the evil which is heralded by a menace.

Graisse pas tini sentiment. Fat has no sentiment.

People often grow stout in spite of misfortunes and distress.

Cé couteau qui connaîte ça qui nans CHÊr *geomou.* It is the knife that knows what is in the heart of the pumpkin.

Haï moune, main pas bâ yeaux pañèn poû châïer dleau. Hate people, but don't give them baskets to fetch water.

That is, do not impute to them crimes that are impossible to their character, and abhorrent to their nature.

Baignèn iches mounes, main pas lavez dêïèr zoréïes yeaux. Bathe people's children, but do not wash behind their ears.

Excess of coddling, and self-identification with respect to, the belongings of others, are here deprecated.

Creole.	*English.*

1 *Jâdin loèn, gombo gâter.* — The garden far, the o<u>chre</u> spoils.

Temps moune connaîte lôte nans grand-joû, nans nouite yeaux pas bisoèn chandelle poû clérer yeaux. — When a person has known another in the day-time, he does not need a candle to recognise him at night.

Our previous knowledge of a person's disposition is a criterion by which to judge of what he is likely to do under given circumstances.

Cé nans temps laplie béf bisoèn lacné *li.* — It is in rainy season that the ox has need of his tail.

Si léphant pas té save boyaux li gouos, li pas sé valer calebasses. — Had the elephant not known the size of his intestines, he would not have swallowed calabashes.

1 *Liane yame ca mârer yame.* — The yam vine ties the yam.

Alluding to the wide-awake ones of the world, who often hang, like Haman, on the gibbets their perfidy had contrived for the undoing of some innocent fellow-creature.

Mamans ca fair iches, main pas cnérs *yeaux.* — Mothers make (beget) children, but not their hearts.

Macaque pas jamain ca die iche li laide. — Monkey never says its young is ugly.

Men regard sometimes with absurd partiality whatever proceeds from them, or is the result of their individual exertions.

Macaque caresser iche li touop, li fourer doègt nans ziex li. — The monkey fondling its young too much, has (at length) poked her finger into its eye.

Macaque connaîte qui <u>bois</u> *li ca monter.* — Monkey knows what <u>tree</u> to climb.

An insolent man is not such to those who could and would chastise him.

Badnèn bien épis macaque; main pouèngâde mañèn laché li. — Joke freely with the monkey; but beware of <u>handling</u> his tail.

Alluding to the well known touchiness of Jacko about his caudal region. Liberties and encroachments may proceed to great lengths; but there is a point at which they rouse the sleeping devil in the meekest of men.

Creole.	*English.*

Misèr ca fair macaque manger piments.   Want makes monkey eat pepper.

The iron pressure of Necessity drives men to concessions foreign to their natural predilections.

Malhèrs pas ca châyer con laplie.   Accidents do not threaten like rain.

Bagyaïe qui fair ziex fair nez.   Whatever affects the eye affects the nose.

Qui méler zéfs nans calenda ouôches ?   What business have eggs in the dance of stones ?

Qui méler rose nans paquet bois Jacques ?   What business has a rose in Jacque's bundle of wood ?

This is to meddlers in matters they know nothing about; to men eager after, and moving in, society which they cannot enjoy without injury or self-abasement; in short, to all who, through their own folly, are, and suffer for being, where they ought not to have intruded.

Pâler touop ca léver chein nans dômî.   Too much talking rouses the watchdog from sleep.

The eager whisperings of irresolute thieves are as sure to produce the result above described, as the babblings and childish indiscretion of some men are to bring ruin on their projects by putting the vigilance of envy on the alert.

Pâler pas rimède.   Talking is no remedy.
Páouôles pas tini coulèr.   Words have no colour.

This is generally said in rebuke of persons who stare a speaker out of countenance.

Faut paouôles môr poû mounes pé vive.   Words must die that men may live.

Very short will be the earthly existence of a person who does not allow slander to die a natural death, but fumes and frets at every thing said against him.

Creole.	*English.*
Ravette pas jamain tni raison dourant poule.	Cockroach never is in the right where the fowl is concerned.

The reign of injustice, during which the insect symbolised the Negro, and the bird, his oppressor, is slowly passing away. There is now some chance for the roach, and day by day he is vindicating his claim to a little more.

Rasiers tini zoreies.	Bush has ears.
Cé souliers tout-sêl qui save si bas tini tous.	Shoes alone know if the stockings have holes.
Tamboû tini grand train páce en-didans li vide.	A drum makes a loud noise because it is empty within.
Tampée ca gañen malhèrs ça doublons pas sa Géri.	A penny buys troubles which doubloons cannot cure.
Travâï pas mal; cé ziex qui capons.	Work is not hard; it is the eyes that are cowards.
Cé lhèr vent ca venter moune ca ouèr lapeau poule.	It is when the wind is blowing that we see the skin of a fowl.

The true character a man can be seen only under circumstances that ruffle the every-day monotony of his life.

Voyer chein, chein voyer laché li.	Send dog, dog sends his tail.

The reference here is to that conceited laziness which likes to obey by proxy.

Nômme mort, zêbes ca lever douvant lapôte li.	The man has died, grass grows before his door.
Si zandoli té bon viâne li pas sé ca driver.	If the lizard had eatable flesh, it would not be so common.

CREOLE TRANSLATIONS, &c.

The following specimens, (which are all we have room for,) are intended to exemplify two modes of translating into Creole. Our first piece, from the Gospel of St. John, is a close translation, which was made, experimentally, from the Latin; and afterwards compared with the Greek. In some verses we have departed from the formula *"answered and said:"* and have substituted *"made for answer,"* or simply *"answered,"* the latter renderings being the only ones allowable in Creole. In the 12th verse, we begin the woman's question with *die moèn*, "tell me," for which there is no equivalent in the English nor French translation; but we think it answers to the interrogatory particle in the original, which is represented in the Latin version by *num.* Our other pieces are paraphrases, more or less free, from Perrin, Æsop and La Fontaine. The last is a sample of Haytian, by M. l'Hérisson, surnamed the Béranger of Hayti.

JOHN IV.—6—19.

Creole.	French.	English.
6. Apouésent, pîts Jacob té nans place là. Jésis, con li té lassc épîs route li, assise bôd pîts la; et côté coté mindi con-ça.	6. *C'était là qu'était le puits de Jacob. Jésus donc, étant fatigué du chemin, s'assit près du puits: c'était environ la sixième heure* du jour.	6. Now Jacob's well was there. Jesus therefore, being wearied with *his* journey, sat thus on the well: *and* it was about the sixth hour.
7. Yon femme, gens Samarie, vinî haler dleau. Jésis dîc li: Bà-moèn boèr.	7. *Une femme samaritaine étant venue pour puiser de l'eau, Jésus lui dit: Donne-moi à boire.*	7. There cometh a woman of Samaria to draw water: Jesus saith unto her, Give me to drink.
8. (Discipes li étant té aller nans boûq la gañèn povisions.)	8. *Car ses disciples étaient allés à la ville, pour acheter des vivres.*	8. (For his disciples were gone away unto the city to buy meat)

9. Alosse, femme sama-
ritaine la dîe li : coument
fair ous, qui yon Juif, ca
mander *dleau* poû boèr
nans lamain moèn, qui
yon femme samaritaine?
pàce Juifs pas ca méler
épis gens Samarie.

9. *Cette femme sa-
maritaine lui répondit :
Comment toi, qui es
Juif, me demandes-tu à
boire, à moi qui suis
femme samaritaine? car
les Juifs n'ont point de
communication avec les
Samaritains.*

9. Then saith the wo-
man of Samaria unto
him, How is it that
thou, being a Jew,
askest drink of me,
which am a woman of
Samaria? for the Jews
have no dealings with
the Samaritans.

10. Jésis fair li poû la
réponse : Si ous té con-
naîte ça Bondié bate, et-
pis qui moune ça qui ca dîe
ous : Bâ-moèn boèr, ous
sé mander, et li sé va bâ
oûs, dleau vivant.

10. *Jésus répondit et
lui dit : Si tu connais-
sais le don de Dieu, et
qui est celui qui te dit :
Donne-moi à boire, tu
lui en aurais demandé
toi-même, et il t'aurait
donné une eau vive.*

10. Jesus answered
and said unto her, If
thou knewest the gift
of God, and who it is
that saith to thee, Give
me to drink; thou
wouldest have asked of
him, and he would
have given thee living
water.

11. Femme la dîe li :
Maîte, ous pas tnî aïen
poû haler dleau èvec, et
pîts la fond ; ainsi, óti ous
tnî dleau vivant la?

11. *La femme lui dit :
Seigneur, tu n'as rien
pour puiser, et le puits
est profond ; d'ou aurais-
tu donc cette eau vive?*

11. The woman saith
unto him, Sir, thou
hast nothing to draw
with, and the well is
deep : from whence
then hast thou that
living water?

12. Dîe-moèn, èce ous
plis grand-tête passé papa
nous Jacob, qui bâ nous
pîts ça-là, óti li-même,
zenfants li, et-pis bêtes
li, té ca boèr?

12. *Es-tu plus grand
que Jacob notre père,
qui nous a donné ce
puits, et qui en a bu lui-
même, aussi bien que
ses enfants et ses trou-
peaux?*

12. Art thou greater
than our father Jacob,
which gave us the well,
and drank thereof him-
self, and his children,
and his cattle?

13. Jésis répône li :
Moune qui ca boèr nans
dleau cela-la, va soèf en-
cot;

13. *Jésus lui répon-
dit : Quiconque boit de
cette eau aura encore
soif;*

13. Jesus answered
and said unto her, Who-
soever drinketh of this
water shall thirst
again :

14. Main ça qui boèr
nans dleau la m'a bâ li,

14. *Mais celui qui
boira de l'eau que je lui*

14. But whosoever
drinketh of the water

pas ca soèf poû jamain ; main dleau la m'a bâ li la, va vinî endidans li yon soûce dleau qui 'a sîmon-ter joûque lavie étênelle.

donnerai n'aura jamais soif, mais l'eau que je lui donnerai deviendra en lui une source d'eau qui jaillira jusqu'à la vie éternelle.

that I shall give him shall never thirst ; but the water that I shall give him shall be in him a well of water springing up into ever-lasting life.

15. Femme la dîe li: Maîte, bâ-moèn dleau cela-la, poû moèn pas soèf encor, ni vinî ici poû haler.

15. *La femme lui dit: Seigneur, donne-moi de cette eau, afin que je n'aie plus soif, et que je ne vienne plus ici pour en puiser.*

15. The woman saith unto him, Sir, give me this water, that I thirst not, neither come hither to draw.

16. Jésis dîe li: Allez, criez mari ous, et-pîs vinî ici.

16. *Jésus lui dit: Va, appelle ton mari, et viens ici.*

16. Jesus saith unto her, Go, call thy husband, and come hither.

17. Femme la fair li poû la réponse: Moěn pas tinî mari. Jesis dîe li: Ous bien dîe: moèn pas tnî mari:

17. *La femme répon-dit: Je n'ai point de mari. Jésus lui dit: Tu as fort bien dit: Je n'ai point de mari;*

17. The woman an-swered and said, I have no husband. Jesus said unto her, Thou hast well said, I have no husband:

18. Pàce ous ja tinî cînq maris, et, apouésent, ça ous tinî la pas mari ous: nans ça cé la vérité ous pâler.

18. *Car tu as eu cinq maris ; et celui que tu as maintenant n'est pas ton mari: tu as dit vrai en cela.*

18. For thou hast had five husbands; and he whom thou now hast is not thy husband: in that saidst thou truly.

19. Femme la dîe li: Maîte, moèn ca ouèr ous cé yon pouophète.

19. *La femme lui dit: Seigneur, je vois que tu es un prophète.*

19. The woman saith unto him, Sir, I per-ceive that thou art a prophet.

FABLES, &c.

Canari et-pîs Chôdièr-fer.

From *Perrin.*

Yon vousse dleau té ca châïer yon chôdièr-fer épîs yon canari aller. Chô-dièr-fer la ca dic baï canari :—"Pas pèr, non, fouèr ; moèn pas câcr fair ous dîtort." Main canari répône li :—" Tempouie, halez-corps-ous loèn moèn, sousplét ; páce, con corps moèn et-pìs cela-ous pas mêmes pièce, pièce, si lâïvièr la jéter ous la-sous moèn, aïo pitit poû moèn ! pisse m'a crasé en mille mïettes."

Mounes qui tinî sentiment pas vlé compànie gens qui forts passé yeaux ni coté poche, ni en grandèr, ni coument coument.

Mouche ét-pîs Béf.

From *Perrin.*

Yon mouche qui té posée la-sous cône yon gouos papa bèf, té pèr bèf la pas té pé sippôter poids li. Alosse, i ca dîe baï bèf:—" Missier, pàdon poû davoèr moèn assise icite ; main si moèn ca péser tête ous touop, díe moèn, et m'a sôtî, poû soulager ous. Béf, apouésent, ca mander :—" Main, ça ca pâler là ?"—" Cé moèn."—" Qui ' moèn' ?"—" Mî moèn ici."—" O ho, cé ous, manzè' mouche ? Pas toublez corps-ous, machèr. Ous pas loûd pièce con ous ca coèr. Moèn pas sé 'a save ous té là, si ous pas té pàler—et lhèr ous sotî la-sous cône moèn, fair-ous coèr moèn pas c'aller sentî lhèr ous aller."

Toute moune cé grand quêchoïe—silon yeaux-même ; main lézôtes là poû jiger ça yeaux yé poû-toute-bon. Qualité yon nômme pas faite pà couéyance li.

Rinâd ét-pîs Baboune.

Paraphrased from Æsop's Fox and Ape.

Temps moèn té jène—jène, jène tit bouaï encor—
Moèn té aimèn lîe fàce louoi Baboune :
Con li gañèn yon royôme pâ belle danse,
Et-pis coument li pède ça pâ bétise.
Toutes bêtes sauvaïes sembler poû féter fète :—
Léphant, lïon, tigue, matapèl, tatou,
Lape, couenque, agouti, biche, pôtepique, ràdène—
Enfin, toutes bêtes Bondié métter nans bois,
Touver yeaux là, farauds con pas possibe.

Moèn pas cêtain qui danser yeaux dânser,
Si té tamboû, o si cété viélon;
Si festin la pouend-coup en-bas yon tente,
Obèn nans caïe, la-sous plancher ciré;
Main moèn connaite, pâmi toutes ces bêtes la,
Cé maîte Baboune qui té plis fine dansèr.
Li "batte lézailes," li "chasser," "déchasser,"
"Tomber en quate," èvec yon grace finie.
Ces lézôtes la, étounèns, châmés, fous,
Applaudî li épîs "bouavo," "hurré;"
Yeaux die : "Ah oui, voélà yon bon dansèr !
Potez couronne poû tête compèr Baboune :
Yon bon dansèr doé fair yon bon louoi!"
Jisse lïon même daccord nans zaffair la.
Et mî Baboune louoi la-sous touône li,
Epîs toute bête parée poû sêvî li!
Malhérêsement, zaffairs la-sous latèr,
Ni ça louoi, ni ça pôr CHocofin,
Toujoûs tinî quêchoïe poû gâter li.
Pâmi sijets louoi Baboune, yon sêl
Tirer tête lî nans bonnete lézôtes la ;—
Cété Rinâd.   Lhèr danser té fini,
Toute respect li poû ouoi Baboune tomber.
Pâce li compouende yon nômme pé fair belles zesses
Sans li connaîte diriger pas lézôtes :
Con-ça, yon joû li bander yon zatrappe,
Et-pîs métter yon gouos papaïe ladans.
Lhèr toute té pouète, li inviter louoi
Poû fair yon toû poû ouèr possessions li.
Temps yeaux river nans zatrappe la, li die :
"Mon ouoi, gâdez, main ça yon belle papaïe !
Malhérêsement, lamain moèn touop boutou
Poû river li."   Baboune pas bâ li temps
Finî esquise li : main, con yon gouos safe,
Li ca lancer poû happer papaïe la.
Zatrappe bandée pas jamain nans sômeî !
Alossa Baboune touver corps-li bien pouis.
Compèr Rinâd, èvec yon lair dédain,
Die li conça; "Rétez là, cher Baboune :

Asïle yon sotte cé là ôti ous yé.
Ous touop couyon poû gouvêner lézôtes."

———

Gens nous content mériter toute baggaïe :
N'a fair yon saint épis yon grand canaïe ;
Main fair con fair, natïe yon nômme va vainque :
Yon saint fôcé va jirer "foute" et "fouenque !"

———

Cigale et-pîs Fômi.

Paraphrased from La Fontaine.

———

Cigale, toute temps soleî té chaud,
    Pas fair dôte choïe, passé chanter.
Ace poû manger, pas yon môceau
    Li pas châcher poû li serrer.

Lhouvênaïe vinî : con-ça, toute bête
    Fourer corps-yeaux nans callefoû yeaux.
Et ça qui té tnî tit lot yeaux faite
    Dîe baîe laplie : " Allez coco !"

Main pôr Cigale, nans tou-bois li,
    Sentî lafaim la-sous dos foète :
Pas yon tit bête, afôce laplîe ;
    Li héler : " Hélas, moèn nans boète !"

Apoués, li chonger dame Fômi,
    Yon voésine nans villaïe li même ;
Poû li, li pas té ca dômî,
    Non-plis chanter nans temps carême.

Nans chaque tit coèn nans tou-tèr li
    Li sembler graines poû temps bisoèn.
Yon joû, pendant yon lembellî,
    Cigale aller mander tit bouin.

Apoués yeaux dîe yone-à-lôte bonjoû,
Cigale coumencer baîe fômî bouche-doû :
—" Machèr macoumèr, moèn vinî ouèr si
Ous sé vlé agî poû touver mêci.

Gàdez ! ous pas ouèr coument moèn changée ?
Moèn fini douboute, et cé fôte manger.
Nans graines ous tni, si ous sé pouéter,
M'a rende ous li doube, lhèr laplie réter."
—"Pouéter ! Main, die, ça ous té ca fair
Pendant carême, lhèr sôlei té clair ?"
—"Poû ça, macoumèr, pas compte mal poû rende :
Nans temps carême gôge moèn pouèsse té fende,
Afôce moèn chanter calendas, bellairs,
Et mille dôtes chanters, bale les travaièrs."
—"Ein hein ! fair belle voix, et pouéter apoués !
Toulouse, machèr, ous tni font épés !
Pisse chanter carême té si bon baggaïe,
Allez danser passer lhivênaïe !"

"Badinez bien avec Macaque."

L'Hérison.

Grand' maman moïn dit : Nans Guinée,
Grand mouché rassemblé youn jour
Toute pêpe li contré nan tournée,
Et pis li parlé sans détour :
" Quand zôt allez foncer nan raque,
Connain coûment grand moune agi :
Badinez bien avec macaque,
Mais na pas magnié queue à li."
. . . .
Grand'mam moïn dit moïn bon qui chose,
Lô li prend bon coup malavoume.*
Li dit moîn con ça : " Monrose,
Nan tout' grand zaffaires faut dit : Houme !"
Maïs peut-on flanqué moïn youn claque,
Ou pitôt terminer ainsi :
Badinez bien avec macaque,
Main na pas magnié queue à li.

---

* That is, *lhèr li té pouend yon bon coûde ouôme*, when she had taken a strong
swill of grog.

ERRATA.

Page 7, *dele* line 10 from bottom, the illustration being incorrect.
  „ 8, lines 3 and 4 from top, for '*fouisé*,' '*frusé*,' read *fouisèe, frusée*.
  „ 9, line 4 from bottom, for '*modre*,' read *mordre*.
  „ 13, lines 5 and 10 from bottom, for 'hiatusses,' read hiatuses.
  „ 16, line 4 from bottom, for '*hades*,' read *hardes*.
  „ 18, „ 17 „ top, for '*ma taute*,' read *ma tante*.
  „ 23, „ 4 „ „ „ '*faramallerd*,' read *faramallero*.
  „ „ „ 10 „ „ „ 'ungraulateud,' " ungranulated.
  „ 27, „ 11 „ bottom, for 'caze,' read case.
  „ 34, „ 13 „ „ „ 'repitition,' read repetition.
  „ „ „ 12 „ „ „ '*chêmber*,' „ сhêmber.
  „ 35, „ 13 „ top „ 'hundred other,' read hundreds *of* other.
  „ „ „ 14 „ „ „ '*motie*,' read *motié*.
  „ 38, lines 7 and 9 from bottom, for '*pît, puit*,' read *pîts, puits*.
  „ 42, line 8 from top, for '*ba*,' read *bâ*.
  „ „ „ 15 „ bottom, for '*doe*,' read *doé*.
  „ 44, „ 6 „ top, for '*travaîe*,' „ *travâî*.
  „ 72, „ 12 „ bottom, for 'utterance them,' read utterance *to* them.
  „ 77, „ 11 „ top, for '*ba*,' read *baîe*.
  „ 79, first line of note, for 'genetive,' read genitive.
  „ 80, line 1 from bottom, for '*ba*,' read *bâ*.
  „ 81, „ 1 „ „ „ '*la moële*,' read *la moelle*.
  „ 83, „ 1 „ „ after 'Is,' read *Goulard's water*.
  „ 86, „ 4 „ „ for '*toûmente*,' read *toûmenté*.
  „ 87, „ 14 „ „ „ 'pronouns,' „ prepositions.
  „ 95, „ 7 „ top, after '*stimar*,' read *la*.
  „ „ „ „ „ „ for '*attérir*,' „ *échouer*.
  „ „ „ 9 „ bottom, „ '*bìen*,' „ *bien*.
  „ „ „ 7 „ „ „ 'eqnivalent,' read equivalent.
  „ 96, „ 8 „ top, „ '*prère*,' read *frère*.
  „ 98, „ 12 „ bottom, „ '*bôte*,' „ *botte*.
  „ 100, „ 6 „ „ „ '*zaffaire, ces affaires*,' read *zaffair, cette*
  „ 102, „ 8 „ top, „ '*corps li*,' read *corps-yeaux*.   [*affaire*.
  „ 104, „ 4 „ bottom, „ '*jilet*,' „ *gilet*.
  „ „ „ 6 „ „ „ 'that of,' „ those of.
  „ 107, „ 11 „ top, „ 'We,' „ They.
  „ 109, „ 11 „ „ „ '*loûer*,' „ *louer*.
  „ 110, lines 9 and 12 from bottom, for '*lever*,' read *léver*.
  „ 111, line 2 from top, for '*vaûmter*,' read *vaûmier*.
  „ „ „ 9 „ bottom, „ '*sementer*,' „ *sêmenter*.
  „ 118, „ 6 „ top, „ '*à-cote*,' „ *à-coté*.
  „ 125, „ 2 „ bottom, „ '*laché*,' „ *laсhé*.